Best wishes
Alex

GLORY DAYS

Alex Askaroff

Country Books

Published by Country Books/Ashridge Press
Courtyard Cottage, Little Longstone, Bakewell, Derbyshire DE45 1NN
Tel: 01629 640670
e-mail: dickrichardson@country-books.co.uk
www.countrybooks.biz
www.sussexbooks.co.uk

ISBN 978-1-910489-43-7 (paperback)
ISBN 978-1-910489-44-4 (hardback)
ISBN 978-1-910489-45-1 (ebook)

© 2017 Alex Askaroff

British Library Cataloguing in Publication Data.
A catalogue record for this book is available from the British Library.

BISAC Subject Headings: Biographical
CIP Library Reference: Biographical

COVER ACKNOWLEDGEMENT
Cover photograph by Sarah Askaroff
Cover design by Tom Askaroff

DEDICATION & ACKNOWLEDGEMENT

I must say a big thank you to all my friends and family who have kept out of the way just enough to let me complete yet another book. Truthfully without their interest and support I would probably take up golf and spend my life chasing a little white ball, catching it and then walloping it away from me again. Yana, my darling wife has once again been my best friend, critic and levelling board. Who knows without her there may have been a lot more swear words in here! A huge thank you to Corrinne, my favourite daughter in law in the whole world. I think that her efforts to improve my English are actually paying off and this book has her magic touch.

A massive thank you to Malcolm Lawson who did the final read through and picked up the last errors with his professional expertise (and made me remove most of my hyphens).

Finally once again to my friend Dick Richardson at Country Books who will hopefully make some sense of all my notes, stories, and inscriptions to build another book that we can be proud of.

Oh, I must add one extra thanks to Priscilla our new Patterdale cross puppy. Without her constant 'help' I would have finished this book at least six months earlier!

ACKNOWLEDGEMENT

The images in this publication are by permission of Alex Askaroff, the people named in the stories that supplied them, or are in the Public Domain. If any copyright holder believes this is not the case Country Books would be pleased to be informed to correct further editions.

Published in Great Britain by Country Books

Second Edition

Printed and bound in Great Britain by

Ebook converted in Great Britain by

CONTENTS

The fabulous Pumpkin Patch in Hailsham is just one of the many shops that I visit which are just a riot of colour and excitement. Many of the shops are run by an enthusiastic workforce that encourage all types of sewing from money saving practical ideas to hobby quilting for passionate retirees.

INTRODUCTION

It seems like a million years ago that I started writing my journals; my little observations on life as it rushed by. At the time I'm sure Raquel Welch was wearing a skimpy leather bikini in some film about cavemen and Jane Fonda was flogging her workout videos. Yet here we are at the start of book eleven – another twisting journey, another chunk of my world, complete with crazy customers. It dawned on me a few years ago that my life can be measured by my books, each one taking several years to build. I am slowly disappearing from this world but I am plastered over countless pages on book shelves all around the globe. If you have never read one of my books before be prepared for a rollercoaster ride through the Sussex countryside.

Life is just as exciting; I am still driving my old banger of a Land Rover, which, over the last 20 years, has travelled almost 240,000 miles along the highways and byways of East Sussex and still never let me down. The phone still rings with customers, some happy to find me still alive and still fixing sewing machines, but some definitely not! "My sewing machine has gone wrong and you have only just fixed it."

"Mrs Berry, you know that I have not been to you for years."
There is a long pause while the tiny cogs of her sneaky brain
revolve. "Well I've hardly used it and I'm not paying you twice!"

One of my customers once asked me how I cope with such a
boring job, doing the same thing over and over again, every day,
year after year. At first I was taken aback, as boring was the one
thing that I have never found my job to be. I explained that no
two days could ever be the same, no two rooms, and no two
customers. One moment I am in some old upholsterer's
workshop, the next in a school somewhere, the next a large
manor or a beaten up housing association flat. As the years fly by
I meet the mad, the sad, and the plain bonkers in equal amounts.

I visit some amazing places, one second I'm in a tenement block on a housing estate the next working I am in the drawing room of some country manor that is a mile down a private drive. My job is like having an 'A-list access all areas pass,' to my area.

Little seems to have changed until I stop and examine my life. I'm older, my hair has faded to grey, my trousers do battle with my waistline, my eyes blur a little more and the doctor prescribe extra pills to pop on a daily basis.

I went on to tell her that I have the best job ever, crazy but true. I explained that it's something to do with my share of larger than life characters. One moment I have Sue on the line in a panic, "I am making banners at the Notting Hill carnival," she shouts over the street music. "My Bernina is skipping stitches, what do I do

Alex, WHAT DO I DO?" Then there was Julie at Camber Sands Holiday Park, "You can't come down today Alex, George Clooney and Matt Damon are filming on the beach and staying at our park. It is mayhem here. Bill Murray was wandering around with hardly a stitch on last night and then they went to Rye for fish'n'chips. They brought the whole town to a standstill. You won't get near the place, Paparazzi are everywhere. OH MY GOD, IT'S GEORGE!" I am left staring at the phone buzzing in my hand. In my mind's eye I could see Julie rushing out of her linen shed while applying lipstick and trying to 'accidentally' bump into the movie star. Heaven only knows how that conversation went.

We often get stars filming in Sussex but when Monuments Men were filming down on Camber Sands the whole area, including Rye where George Clooney, Matt Damon and Bill Murray bought their fish & chips, came to a standstill. They used the beaches as they are similar to the Normandy beaches.

I was at a farm near Peasmarsh when a helicopter went up, over and down. "That's Paul McCartney's ex," said my customer with a snarl. "She can't be bothered to drive the mile so she gets flown from her house to Paul's!" Then there was Sarah who works for Glyndebourne Opera, almost in tears, "If we can't finish the costumes the rehearsal for Aida will be cancelled. You have to come out right now, please hurry. I'll have a pass waiting for you at security." The same has happened at schools now where the exams are timed to coincide all over the country. It is apparently to cut out cheating in this world of instant communications. The problem is that if a machine goes wrong during one of these exams, panic sets in immediately as the school only has a limited time before the exams stop and it does not matter how good the pupil is, without their machines to conjure up their magic it will be a fail.

For years there was a multimillion pound business in my area making curtains and supplying fabrics. The boss would glide into work in his precious and highly polished Rolls Royce and stop in his allotted place clearly marked 'Managing Director'. On the day I was fixing his sewing machine I just pulled into it as it was the closest place to the machine I needed to fix. He wasn't there anyway so I thought I would be safe. The machine, purpose built in Italy, was a work of art; the size of a room and controlled by a computer operator in one corner. The monster made quilts to order of any size, fabric and thickness from a single summer quilt to a queen sized beauty with its own individual quilted pattern of choice.

When the beast went wrong everyone in the factory held their breath and drew lots as to who would break the bad news to the boss. Before I used to fix the machine they had to fly in an engineer from the factory in Italy and put him up for a few days while he worked on it. Sometimes the machine would be out of action for weeks and the final bill always ran into thousands. The boss was over the moon when he found me, who fixed his monster for a few quid. One day when I was fixing his machine the boss arrived to find someone parked in his allotted spot. He flew into a rage and I could hear the commotion as he came through the factory, demanding to know who had parked in his place. All I could hear was him shouting as he got closer and closer. I was unaware of what it was all about until he got to the offices next to the sewing machine. "DOES ANY OF YOU KNOW WHO HAS PARKED IN MY BLOODY SPACE?" There was a silence before one of the girls squeaked out, "I think it was Alex, sir."

"ALEX, WHO THE HELL IS ALEX."

"He is fixing your quilter in the next room, sir." A sticky silence followed.

"Oh Alex, yes I see, yes Alex…, good work, carry on everyone." He left without another word and I didn't need to slide down the pipe outside the loo window! When I got back to my car there was a little hand written note from him telling me to feel free to use his space any time I needed it. I think that I was one of the only people in Sussex that he was always polite to.

Nelda Sale is on the line: "Your onscreen presence has a lot of energy." She had watched some of my You Tube clips on old sewing machines. I wasn't sure what she meant by my 'screen presence' but took the compliment. "We are filming the next series of The Great British Sewing Bee for the BBC, what are the chances of you doing a few spots for us? We need someone to teach Claudia Winkleman how to sew." I explained to the producer that she had more chance of seeing me walk on water and dance the Nutcracker in a ballet costume before politely declining her offer. For over 20 years I have turned down proposals from every television and film company as I gently protected my introvert status. As you will find out later on, it all went horribly wrong and I did get my fifteen seconds of fame, or rather infamy.

My job is a whirlwind of new faces and new places. "It's Steven, you know Steven Caine from Tom Bag."
"Hi Steven, what can I do for you?" It was Sunday evening and way past my bedtime. A cold feeling of dread was creeping over me. "We have an order for 1,200 bags for the new Star Wars movie, The Force Awakens."
"Oh, well done Steven, that's great business."
"No it's a nightmare, both industrials have just packed up and we have to finish the order by Tuesday. We have been working around the clock. Can you come out and sort the machines?"
"Yes of course, I can come after I have finished my booked in customers tomorrow evening."
"No now, we need you now. Everything has come to a halt and we are all running around like chickens with a fox after them. We are in meltdown, what is Harrison Ford going to say if he doesn't get his personalised bag from us? I'll brew some fresh coffee, I've already sent a taxi. It should be outside any moment!"

Ingrid Prior is in a state of nervous excitement. "It's for the Royal Opera House. I have 24 tutus to finish and all my machines have broken. Broken I tell you-Kaput!"

"But Ingrid, last time I visited you had six. They can't all have broken!"

"You tell the machines that. They have all expired from exhaustion, one after the other, the last one just went bang and now we're stuck. How soon can you get here?" Her voice was tinged with apprehension and dread. It looked like my Sunday morning was going to be a trip to Hastings.

"What is Ridley Scott going to do without his space suits? He's off to Budapest at the end of the week and if we keep 20TH

It's hard to explain how many different trades are touched by sewing from corset makers (who now seem to sell more corsets to men than women) to Doris in Brighton making waistcoats for ferrets. There has been a revival in sewing from period re-enactments to period costume. Here is Sandy and Jim Wotton looking ready for action. The world of sewing has never been so exciting from just getting dressed up for fun to haute couture for a high society bash.

There are loads of new fashions and 'glammed up' Steampunk is on a roll. Steampunk is a relatively new fashion that has taken hold. It is a mix of Victorian and a little of whatever you fancy. Most of these costumes are complex and unique. They have to be made to measure. Here is Karen and Kevin Hardy parading on Eastbourne Pier.

Century Fox waiting we're all in trouble." Nic Miners was desperately trying to soften me up for her company, Robert Allsopp's in Croydon. They specialise in props and clothing for the entertainment industry and somehow managed to drop two machines out of the back of one of their vans. They were making the white space suits for the latest blockbuster, The Martian. Without their machines they were helpless.

It's not always a mad rush though. Carzana Interiors near Lamberhurst book me to service their machines when they have a special order for a special customer. Last time it was the luxury hotel just off Bond Street, Claridges in London. Liz gets all her machines perfect so that she can create beautiful work for the stunning Art Deco hotel.

My life seemed to be like that, I was in a trade with very few experts and in my corner of the world I had become an essential cog, servicing the last remaining industry that had survived the onslaught of cheaper manufactured imports. Lindsey is in a state of pure panic, verging on hysteria and she is on the other end of the telephone. She runs a business called Spoonangel that makes bunting for special occasions, "I can't wait till Thursday, we need the bunting for Jamie Oliver's food festival this weekend. What will he say when he arrives and there is no bunting! Please come out now, please, please."

I know I'm not single-handedly keeping manufacturing going in my corner of the country but sometimes it sure feels like it, countless thousands of machines for countless businesses, decades of dedication quietly oiling the wheels of industry. I often fancy that one day I will pull into my drive and there will

One of my lovely customers, Glenys Whitehead. She learnt her trade at Wenston Manufacturing after leaving school at 14. By 1943 her mum had saved up £26 (half a year's salary) and bought her a new Singer 15k so that she could work at home as well. Wenston's were in Uxbridge, Middlesex and supplied some of the top fashion houses in London. Glenys specialised in 'high fashion blouses'. The team of factory girls often had a sing-song as they sewed away and the owners took them on outings and picnics. She refers to those happy years in the factory, when she was a carefree girl, as her glory days.

be an immaculately dressed old couple waiting by my front door. It will be Queen Liz and hubby. They will have a little medal for me and a slip of paper to put on my wall. I'll make tea before they whip off to their next appointment. I'll pin up my piece of paper and just think to myself 'if only dad could see me now.' I have stayed the course, from the day as a kid when he broke the news that, instead of being a surgeon, as I had dreamed of, the only operating I would do would be on his sewing machines. How proud he would be, he would grab me and kiss each cheek with his stubbly, bristled face and hug me until I couldn't breathe, just as he used to do when he had not seen me for a while. I would blush, and secretly love every second.

I have never moved away from the place where I was born, my hometown of Eastbourne. I have seen the seasons come and go; spring comes, the grass grows, winter arrives, the world rolls on. In recent years, as I tend to my little patch of heaven, we have witnessed extraordinary events with the mass migration of humans. In the 1990's millions of disillusioned British left the country, leaving a huge hole in the economy. Now, with the new freedom of movement in Europe, and wars in the Middle East, families pour in to our island home in enormous numbers. The extra youth and vibrancy they bring has brought many more interesting days. I still remember the beautiful Russian shot-putter with a voice deeper than Tom Jones. She pushed a ten pound note into my hand after all my hard work getting her machine up and running. It was a quarter of what I had asked for. "This is what I pay you," she said in her deep growl. A face off followed as I summed up all my professionalism, learnt from a lifetime of dealing with customers. I stared at her for a good three seconds before folding like a wimp, grabbing the money, and making a dash for the car. A tenner was better than having to tell my wife I had been beaten up by a woman!

I travel my daily rounds in my old banger, fixing machines and picking up my stories, whether it is about Elvis's daughter in Rotherfield or some old war story; like the fruits in my garden I carefully gather them up one by one.

Boring! That is the one word in the dictionary that I could never use to describe my job. If my job was a piece of string with

The day I called to service the machines at Eastbourne College they were putting on a fashion show. All the dresses were made from second hand maps from charity shops and looked simply amazing.

boring at one end, right at the other would be me, running like a crazy thing, as far away from it as possible. Sussex is changing fast but I still adore living among the ruins of our lost Empire, driving down the endless tiny lanes to yet another customer, yet another tale.

The fact that so many people keep urging me to carry on writing also spurs me on. What started all those years ago as a simple Millennium Calendar with a compilation of stories has grown and grown. The first journal of my life, Patches of Heaven, was a huge risk and a step into the unknown but the book was so well received that I sold out within a few weeks (even with the spelling mistakes!). All these years later it seems to be a natural

Annie Smith used to run from the Germans shooting the sheep and cattle in Eastbourne. She is 94 here and holding up 'Have I Got A Story For You' that I wrote some years back. She told me that she reads it when she needs a smile.

course of events for me to write down my experiences as I go.

A while back, just after I had completed and launched 'Have I Got A Story For You', I bumped into a professional proof reader.

Bobby Stewart is an expert machinist. For friends and family she makes some amazing period costumes out of anything from curtains to tablecloths. Here is Tony Harris dressed as our most infamous king Henry VIII. Picture by Simon Newbury.

"I've never read anything like it," he told me with an ominous tone, "No structure, no theme, and you wander off topic more than an old woman in a nursing home."

"So you're not my number one fan then?" I laughed.

"I loved it," he retorted, "It may just have been the best book I've ever read. I am already half way through my second read. If you were famous it would probably be on the best sellers list and criticised all to hell. It's crazy and brilliant all at the same time, for Christ's sake you even have a recipe for a pizza in there! You wouldn't mind signing my copy for me while you're here, would you? Just in case you crack it and make the big time."

The most amazing affect I have ever had was on a sweet old Londoner called Doll. I had called on Dorothy Sullivan, who lived in Langney at the time, to service her machine. While I was there all the stars aligned and out poured a wonderful tale from her youth. I visited her several times to get the whole story right. It was about her years' hop picking and all the exciting times she had. I called her story 'Spies & Spitfires', much of it taking place during the Second World War on the Sussex/Kent border. After I had finished the book, 'Tales From The Coast', which had her story in it, I took her a copy. About a year went by and her son came round to pick up some more copies for her relatives. He told me that she had fallen in love with the story of her past, reading it over and over. She then made the momentous decision to sell up and move back to where she had lived the best years of her life. I could not believe my ears, Doll had up-sticks and moved house, all because of me putting pen to paper.

As time rolls by I have come to realise that my glory years are slipping quietly away, you know those wonderful years we take for granted where health and energy allows us to go almost anywhere we fancy and do most of the things we want to. If I am spared (we all know life comes with no guarantee), in a decade I should be touching my six score years and ten. Age has given me the knowledge that these days are priceless, unique, and so quickly gone forever.

On the positive side I enjoy every moment, even when I am in a bad mood. It sounds crazy I know, but true all the same. I guess it's all about attitude and realising how quickly time passes. That was thanks to my dad.

My dad was a terrible sceptic, his half Russian blood had corrupted his soul and to him the glass was always half empty. I asked him why once. He just replied "Read our literature, listen to our songs, we Ruskies glory in the struggle. Of course the glass is half empty, it could be no other way." Like all moody and melancholic Russians, he only seemed to be happy when he was sad. I did look at their literature and listened to their songs – everybody dies! Often, as I went to bed as a kid, dad, ever the pessimist, said to me more than once that if he did not make it through the night, I had money in the bank and two strong legs to carry me through life.

Strangely, his negative outlook on life triggered in me a fascination with time (probably as I waited for his 'good days'). With it came the understanding that we are all unstoppably passing through life. I came to realise that a simple change of attitude can make our predictable daily routine, our Ground Hog Days, anything but boring.

Unlike my dad, this made me determined to grab every second

out of each day, the good and bad, squeezing every ounce out of them. The best thing is, when we make a complete balls up of a day, we have the chance to make a better one every 24 hours! Amazing really when you stop and think about it.

So here we go again, Book 11 is another whirlwind trip of awesome tales and adventures. The stories may not be exactly how they all happened but more importantly to me, it is how I remember them. Hang on to your hats, grab a flask and follow me through the pages of a few of my glory days..

Queen Victoria and Mr John Brocklehurst MP are actually Carole & Leslie Allman. They are performing street artists and for authenticity they sew their fabulous costumes with a 19th century Willcox & Gibbs chain stitch machine.

Leslie also dresses as a 19th Century London street trader to sell apples and oranges.

ROUND AND ROUND

I'm a little ball bearing in a glass jar,
However hard I try I never get too far,
Not a weak link, like the one that's bound to fail,
More of a puppy that likes to chase its tail,
I run around in circles trying to catch up,
Stocking up the larder, filling up my cup,
Though, hard as I try, to get that bit ahead,
I know I'll be that bearing until I drop dead.

A I A

Birth of a King

It was 22nd July 2013 and roasting. I was driving down the coast road in my banger of a Land Rover on my way to Maisy, my last customer of the day. For the last three weeks I had been busily trying to raise enough money to pay for the MOT on my old girl. She had faultlessly taken me through snow, ice and storm for another year but, as usual, had failed. They had welded, bolted and tested her and the bill was £509. With the money that I had earned during the day plus my savings over the last few weeks I was still short, but optimistic. If all went well with Maisy, I should have almost enough to settle the bill and be on my way for another year.

Every self-employed person will know what a job it is to juggle our earnings to cover the bills. In the end I have survived on my own for a quarter of a century and I was proud of it. I rely on no one, standing on my own two feet every day of every week. I have the feeling that is one of the reasons that self-employed people have a bit of a 'cocky' attitude that is sometimes taken the wrong way.

It was hot. Really hot, 35 Celsius in the shade and the car was pushing through the heat like a spoon through a bowl of porridge. In the sun you could add several degrees to the sweltering heat. Only a few days before, it had struggled to reach 12 Celsius with bitter winds as the winter dragged on and on, but today was something else, summer had arrived with a bang. By African standards it was a cool day at the office but today was the warmest day in England for over seven years and had caught us all by surprise. A warm front pushed up from the Sahara had turned Eastbourne into a town straight out of a holiday poster.

I was cruising with all my windows open, dropping down from the hills above Eastbourne. I chased swifts as they scooped along the roads picking up insects, fleeing the farmer's blades as tractors cut the long grass for winter feed. I twisted my way through the winding wooded road, passed the allotments tucked into the side of the hill and then along by my old school, St Bede's, where I used to run amuck along the creaking corridors. I drove by the Hydro Hotel where its lace and linen regulars were roasting on the lawns, probably complete with salmon and cucumber sandwiches, their corners curling in the heat.

Western Lawns was heaving. The Jürgen Matthes students, shipped in en-masse for the summer, were out in force throwing Frisbees and kicking balls. The girls were basting in the sun, while the boys posed doing all sorts of manly things. I knew from experience that later in the day nurses at our local hospital would be slapping soothing ointment on many burnt, pulsating bodies – with little sympathy.

It was high tide and the sea was lazily lapping at the pebbles like an old dog laps at its water bowl. In the reflected haze the water was the colour of blueberry milkshake and flowed seamlessly away into the distance where the fishing boats blended with the horizon, which in turn blurred into a hazy sand colour in the shimmering heat.

There was no wind, the flags flopped lifelessly against the poles like drunks leaning on lamp posts. In the sticky heat tourists bent over the blue railings, staring aimlessly out to sea in a classic seaside scene. Time moves slowly on sizzling days like these. The seagulls, temporarily ejected from their normal beachside residence, were bobbing up and down on the millpond sea. They were just a few yards from shore, watching the sudden spectacle strewn across their shoreline and keeping a beady eye out for any tourist silly enough to leave food within attacking distance. The older gulls had mastered their sweeping dives, taking with them sandwiches and even nicking the tops of ice creams held in kids' hands.

Traffic was slow and I ground to a halt. I was glad of the rest. It had been a long working day starting with a tricky call earlier, which had sent my pulse racing. I had called at a semi-detached in Seaford not far from the cliffs from where Eastenders star Paul Bhattacharjee had decided to leap to his death just a few days earlier. The Saturday after I had been idly spinning for bass below where he had jumped when I heard a scream. I looked around to see two police officers dragging a girl away from the cliff edge. She cried all the way to the waiting van and I said a quiet 'thank you' as she would have landed just feet away from me. Cliffs are always a draw for those desperate few.

So, there I was, working away in my customer's semi when I needed to get a part from my car. I walked out and found the correct part from the thousands that I travel around with and went back in. Only one problem. I went into the wrong front door! I had walked into the neighbours' door. I was concentrating so much on the part and how to fix it into the sewing machine that I had opened the wrong front door, which was exactly the same, and only a few feet away from the correct one.

I walked along the hallway, looked up and stopped. It was like some sort of weird dream, in a parallel universe. Things looked the same but different; there was no sewing machine in the living room, no customers, no television on, no cup of tea on the table. In fact even the table looked different. I went blank unable to comprehend what had happened. I had entered another world that sent my mind spinning. I retraced my steps and walked back out of the house to look at it from the outside. My customer's husband was leaning on his open front door frame with a huge smile. "Had a nice visit did you? Were Sally and Tony pleased to see you? I saw you from my window, heading for the wrong door, but I got there too late just to see you disappear inside. What did they say?"
"Nothing. I didn't see anyone in there." I laughed nervously. "Mind you, it made my mind explode for a few seconds."

Once in the right house we saw the neighbours hanging out the washing together in their back garden. Tony was carefully putting the pegs on as Sally handed him each piece of washing. They had no idea that I had just paid them a visit, but by the way the husband of my customer was leaping about with excitement, I bet he was going to tell them as soon as I had gone. As I fixed the

24

sewing machine I calmed down. On such a hot day I did not need anymore excitement like that! I pocketed my first cheque and hit the road.

Back along Eastbourne seafront the sun had brought out the 'Sunday Drivers' for a three-mile cruise along their regular seafront route. I didn't mind, the traffic gave me a break, and time to soak up the scene. The old Eastbourne drivers who have the average age of Adam and Moses combined often cause havoc with 'White Van Man' and his many colleagues. They normally buzz up and down the seafront roads maintaining the countless eating establishments, bars and hotels that provide them with much of their trade. Moreover the pedestrian traffic lights were constantly flicking to red as people poured onto the beaches like treacle over a warm sponge pudding.

Coming the other way in his large lorry, was my mate Dave. He was waving madly at me from his cab and as we got closer he shouted out of the window, "Bloody tourists! It has taken me forty minutes to get from the leisure pool to here. I'll be home late again tonight. Fancy some mackerel fishing later?"
"You bet," I shouted back, "How about Langney Point at eight?"
"See you there."

Seaweed, thrown out of the sea by angry waves only days before, was rotting along the high tide line. Flies buzzed around it as if celebrating death as all life in the weed slowly perished in the heat. Sea lice, shrimp and a thousand other tiny creatures that normally live on the weed were baking in the relentless sun.

My skin was glistening from the unexpected heat and my shirt was sticking to my hot body. A lifeguard, with a perfect tanned physique, obviously copied from mine, was taking money from a fat lady who was overflowing one of the thousands of deck chairs hastily thrown up along the promenade. Her husband was waving his hands, full of suntan cream, gesturing to the lifeguard that 'the wife' was paying. I laughed to myself because I know how difficult it is to get out of those contraptions and I could almost see her flapping around later as she tried to get up from her deckchair to get to her hotel for an early dinner.

Eastbourne was transformed and glistened like a well oiled bodybuilder. Over the last century our town has perfected the seaside dance, the pleasurable milking of the tourists, which in turn keeps our shops and hotels open for business. What I was seeing here has probably been repeated in most tourist towns in most countries on the planet. What's more is we love it and so do they. Next year many will be back for another break in one of our famous hotels and a stroll down our fabulous Victorian seafront, the jewel in Eastbourne's fading crown.

As I reached the end of Grand Parade I saw a band of thick cloud out towards Bexhill, where I was headed. This was the perfect day for a thunderstorm. A day that the ants all take to the air and provide a feast for the birds on the wing. Even the seagulls will join the air dancing, carrying out ridiculous acrobatics, as they gobble down the unexpected offerings normally hidden well out of reach beneath the soil.

I spotted Frank Richardson in his old Bedford van coming the other way and waved. He waved back with his usual toothy grin. Frank is one of our local characters. He had been driving around in his hand-painted green van since the 1960's. He was an upholsterer by trade but now well retired. He loves his old banger, which has become a 'local celebrity'. His number plate, 847 NPO, is well known around town and he has had the van so long that he has been around the clock in it several times. I remember well the times that my dad would drive to his outworkers with me sitting in the passenger seat of his old Bedford the same as Frank's. I would help him unload all the bits of fabric, filling and trims that we would leave with women all over Eastbourne, then a week later we would collect the sewn up goods. The family's baby business is long gone but the memories are still as fresh as a daisy. The speedo in our Bedford went all the way up to an earth-shattering 70mph, though I doubt the van was capable of that speed, unless the brakes failed and it rolled over Beachy Head! At one time my dad's and Frank's were the only two green Bedford long wheelbase vans in Eastbourne. Frank once joked to me that he was going to try and get in to the next 'Concourse' car event at Western Lawns. That would be so funny as I am sure his van is held together with little more than string, Dulux gloss green and willpower.

Frank had been married longer than anyone that I knew and I once asked him his secret. He just said, "When the storm clouds come-a-blowing, I stay in the garden." I knew what he meant; behind his workshop he had another shed where he spent countless hours painting local scenes. He gave me his favourite one last time I saw him. It is an oil painting of his old shop along Seaside. He is standing in the doorway with all his wares displayed on his forecourt. I had pestered him for years for it as it captured a bit of old Eastbourne, now long gone.

Within the hour I was driving up the long gravel track to Maisy's house, well manor really. It was straight out of a Hitchcock murder mystery. I spotted Maisy in the grounds. She had a Sussex trug under one arm and some secateurs in the other hand. As I drove closer I realised, much to my horror, that she was wearing an old gardening apron and little else! What a sight. It did not make my eyes bleed but I was certainly turning as pink as the sweet peas that she had in her wild tussled hair. I had passed a pot of pink and blue ones back down the drive, probably picked from her garden. They were for sale outside her large iron gates. I adore Maisy, she has the highly contagious 'happiness disease' and a dirty laugh that fell straight out of a beer barrel.

"Too hot to be dressed up today," Maisy shouted, as I rolled to a crunching halt on the gravel. I smiled and tried not to stare at her but her wrinkled knees were something else! "Maisy you're going to get arrested walking around like that."
"Oh no Alex, I have my apron on. Last night I was gardening in the nuddy! Now that could get me arrested, but it was worth it. How many times a year can we be outside in England and it be so warm that we can strip? Not many dear, not many. So as soon as it was dark I crept out of the back door and spent an hour throwing snails over my garden hedge into the fields. I know they will be back by next week but the exercise is fun. I feel like I am adding to their evolutionary development by teaching them how to fly! I throw them underarm now as I can't throw them like I used to, but I do have a mean swing when I send the little darlings sailing through the air. Last week," giggled Maisy, "I threw a beautiful one over the hedge. It had a yellow swirl running around its shell. Well last night it was back. It looked up at me in a rage and demanded to know why I had thrown it!"

"Maisy," I laughed, "You know you're bonkers, don't you?"

"Oh Alex it's the best way to be. When it started to rain last night, lovely warm summer rain, I danced around the lawn without a stitch on. It was so beautiful. I'm no flower fairy mind. Ooh, I see your kiss curls are out!"

"Maisy you're going to make me blush again. It's this damp heat, my hair curls up like a pig's tail."

"Well it looks quite kissable," giggled Maisy like a teenager. "Even though I notice that you have more grey hair than black now. You come in and sort my sewing machine and I'll put some trousers on so that you aren't so shocked. I would think that at your age you had seen it all."

"Hey Maisy, I might have seen it all but I'm not so sure I want to see it again!" We both laughed but I made sure I walked in front of her!

"Can you feel it Alex?"

"The heat? Yes it's suffocating."

"No, the electricity in the air. Look, it's all around you. Look at the swallows circling so high, see the queen ants in the grass. This is a special day, there is energy everywhere."

"It will be special if I catch a nice bass tonight when I go fishing," I added as I got to the front door.

As I walked through the grand old door a wall of stink hit my nose. In the heat it was stifling and Maisy saw my face. "Oh that's only my rotten swede boiling. I noticed that it had gone off in the heat so I decided to boil it up for my supper. I know it smells appalling but once it is smothered in butter it will be just the ticket. Waste not want not!"

Her manor was a dream, beautiful but dilapidated. In the hall was a broken chair with a one-legged doll sitting by it staring straight at me. We walked through a huge room that had oak parquet flooring and may have once been a ballroom as the floor felt sprung, though it may just have been rotten underneath. Huge windows stretched from the floor to the ceiling, some with ripped curtains hanging on broken rails. Mirrors adorned the walls, making the room seem even larger and more magnificent. Each room that we walked through was in a similar state of disrepair. I'm sure that was how Maisy loved it. She had created her own dream world. She looked round at me as I was gawping at the amazing rooms and saw my expression. "Oh don't worry, my kids can squabble over the lot when I am being pushed into the oven at Eastbourne Crem. That's if I don't have a big bonfire and take it all with me!"

"I'll have one of your mirrors Maisy. Mind you it is way too big to get it into my house, I'll have to have it in the garden."

As we arrived at the sewing machine, which was sitting on a small table looking lost in its grand surroundings, Maisy started to sing, *"My baby's gone down the plug 'ole, my baby's gone down the drain. The poor little thing was so skinny and thin he could have been bathed in a pineapple tin."*

I started nodding my head to her song when she suddenly stopped. "I've lost four dress sizes in one year. It is the will of God. He has saved me. This time last year I was a size 22 and just sat in my wheelchair rotting away. That is why this place has become such a dump. Then I became diabetic, which may not sound like fun but I am now down to a size 14 and I even have the use of my arms back. That's why you are here, I need to alter my clothes. I've found a whole room full of them that I'd forgotten all about and they all need altering, well the ones that

30

the moths haven't got. They do so love cashmere and silk. The sewing machine has hardly been used since you last came many years ago but now it is going to get a work-out and I want it perfect. Would you like a nice long glass of something cool?"

"Oh yes please Maisy, anything would be nice today."

"Iced tea it is then." With that she danced off, barefooted through a small servants door in the corner, singing as she went, *"My baby's gone down the plug 'ole, my baby's gone down the drain."* As she moved further away her singing became a faint echo, bouncing along the dusty corridors. *"The poor little thing was so skinny and thin he could have been bathed in a pineapple tin."*

I was left in silence staring out one of the huge windows that overlooked a dilapidated patio with a low stone balustrade. In the garden, broken ornaments dotted the overgrown flowerbeds. Maisy was a strange old girl. When I first met her I remember staring into her wild sea-grey eyes, getting lost in her rambling tales of India and her travels abroad. Now her eyes had dimmed but not her eccentric ways, which she obviously had enough income to indulge. Along the edge of the windowsill lay an assortment of dead insects. Sadly most of them were pointing towards the garden with their heads up to the glass. Each tiny life slowly expired staring at the garden that they so longed to reach, trapped by an invisible shield invented by humans, called glass.

I caught some movement out of the corner of my eye and fluttering through the huge room came a beautiful Red Admiral butterfly. It must have flown in the open door and followed us along the passages. It fluttered around the room and was picked out in the summer light pouring through the dusty windows. It was entrancing and I could almost imagine the tiny creature magically transforming into the old lady of the manor, a ghost from ages past. It did a circle beneath the chandelier like the star of the dinner party before heading for one of the huge windows. It hit the glass and panicked, fluttering madly up and down trying to get out, leaving tiny wing prints on the glass. I looked at all the dead creatures on the sill below and decided that I would open the window and let it out. The windows were enormous and split into two, large Georgian, glazed sash panels. In front of the windows were built-in wooden seats where you could sit and gaze out onto the manicured lawns while perfecting your tapestry or painting.

I climbed up onto one side of the painted wooden benches and wiggled the old brass sliding catch until it slid across. I then pulled on the top sash window but it would not budge. I switched to the lower window and saw a bit of movement so I heaved upwards with all my strength. With a grating slide, it slowly yielded to my efforts. Eventually I had it nearly all the way to the midway point, plenty of room for me to climb out of the window if I had wanted to and enough for the silly butterfly to make a bid for freedom.

Typically the butterfly was now on the other side of the room ignoring my attempts to set it free. I whisked across the room and started flapping my arms at the insect, trying to make it head for the open window and freedom. Eventually after a lot of chasing and flapping the red admiral flitted out of the window into the garden. I watched it circle over the lawn and then a house martin plucked it out of the air! "Crap!" I muttered to myself. What a complete waste of time, and I'd helped to kill it. I started to wiggle the window down when I heard something snap in the frame. It was one of the cords holding the hidden weights which helped the windows to slide up and down. All of a sudden I was holding up the weight of the window, trying not to let go in case it crashed down and smashed the glass panels. It was at this point that Maisy walked in with a silver tray with two glasses and a jug of iced tea, surrounded by an assortment of biscuits. Luckily for me she had slipped some clothes on as well. "What on earth are you doing Alex?"

"I let a butterfly out of the window but the cord has broken. I am not sure what to do, if I let go it might drop and break."

"Hang on, hold it up there, I'll get my broom." Maisy put down the tray and rushed out of the room, returning seconds later with her broom. She jammed it diagonally into the open window. "Now carefully let go and let's see what happens." Luckily for me the broom did the trick and the window wedged open. I sighed and stepped down shaking my aching arms. "I am so sorry Maisy."

"Don't say another word. I should have had those windows sorted years ago. I'll get Yuri, my handyman, to look at it as soon as he gets here. He's from Kiev you know. I found him sleeping in my potting shed two summers ago. Yuri had spent six months travelling across Europe before ending up in my garden, penniless. We came to an understanding, he was so good at fixing things and gardening, that I eventually bought him a van and found him work as a handyman around my friend's houses. He now helps me around here for two days a week for free. He's a marvel. It would not surprise me if he ended up a rich man in a country like ours that rewards hard work. I'll get him to lower the window and lock it and then we will leave it for another year. I would nail it shut myself but Yuri does not trust me with a hammer. He told me that as soon as I have a hammer in my hand everything starts to look like a nail! I go a bit nutty looking for something to whack! At least the butterfly escaped."

"Well, err, actually," I said sheepishly, "One of your House Martins ate it!"

We both started to giggle, "that's life," sniggered Maisy through her nose. "Time for tea."

After a while Maisy left me and I was once more alone in the grand old place. Along the corridor drifted beautiful piano music from Radio 3. The sound was amplified by the large rooms and I started to wonder what sound system Maisy had as it was impressive. Everything in her mansion was quality, much of it broken but quality all the same. It was probably Bang & Olfsen or Bose, and as I had finished the sewing machine, I decided to find Maisy and ask her. I wandered down the dusty corridors towards the sound of the radio and found my way into a large room. In the middle of the empty room was a Steinway piano shining like a black diamond. Maisy was seated at the piano playing. There was no radio, it was her. Her hands were gliding over the keys, rising and falling, caressing each one like a lover caresses the neck of the person they love. Her head was tilted slightly back and her eyes closed. Her face had a wonderfully contented look. I was speechless and watched quietly as Maisy played like a concert pianist.

Maisy opened her eyes and saw me. She smiled, "Frederick Chopin, Ballade Number One. He finished it in 1835," she shouted over the music. With that she closed her eyes and continued. The music slowed to a deep melancholy that echoed through the old manor then it sped up until her hands were a blur.

Then the music became tense and dramatic, suddenly it was humorous then once again passionate. Maisy was taking me on a journey of discovery through the ivory keys of her piano and then in an instant it was all over. "I practice every day at this time. I have to keep my fingers supple in case I am ever asked to perform again. Though I doubt it, most people think that I died years ago."

"Maisy that was simply wonderful, almost spiritual."

"Alex that is exactly right. I once tried to make my students understand that. We are all animals but humans have spirit, something that animals don't and one of the best expressions of that spirit is music, beautiful music. Humans have a lot of flaws but they also have some wonderful attributes and occasionally someone special like Chopin or Mozart or Ronnie Wood comes along and makes us realise we can be something extraordinary. How is my sewing machine going?"

"All perfect." I replied, "It will be good for another few years yet."

"Lovely. Now, I need to get back in the garden and finish off my pruning. Is a cheque all right for you?"

"That's fine Maisy, nearly everyone pays me by cheque these days."

As I drove back out of the long driveway I waved to Maisy who was already back in the garden with her pruning shears. She shouted to me, "There's a storm coming Alex, I can feel it, and a king!" I stopped the car. That was not the usual farewell and it ground me to a halt as I tried to fathom what Maisy said.

"What on earth are you talking about Maisy?"

"There will be a new king born today, full moon rising you see. Before long we shall have another royal, mark my words it's all written in the stars. To be a good ruler a Cancerian would be perfect; thoughtful and kind, caring and protective, all just right for a future king."

I smiled, of course a very pregnant and overdue Kate, once a commoner like us, but now, Her Royal Highness The Duchess of Cambridge, had quietly slipped into St Mary's Hospital in Paddington early in the morning. It was also a strange fact that more things happen during a full moon, including births. Midwives know all about 'full moon babies'. Some justify this by saying that it is simply gravity and as we are all made up of so much water we are obviously affected when the moon is at its strongest. The moon can move trillions of gallons of water so it is bound to have an effect on our bodies. Others say it is much deeper than that and the full moon has a special draw that cannot be so easily explained.

The Duchess' baby was imminent so Maisy would probably be right. Parliament had been busy, playing with ancient laws, clearing the way for the new arrival, be it a boy or girl, so that they could eventually become King or Queen of England. Once the new baby was here, they would be third in line to the throne. Through their veins would flow not only the blood of royalty but also of bank clerks and miners, servants and sailors. Kate was bringing fresh blood to our Kingdom.

I waved and drove on, wondering how Maisy could possibly know that Kate would be having her baby today and a boy! However I had come to learn a long time ago to listen to some of my old customers who acted quite mad but seemed to know so much. As I left the drive I had the feeling that she was just waiting for me to get out of sight before she took her clothes off again! What a priceless darling. She is one of the countless reasons I have the best job in the world.

I stopped up the lane to count my earnings. There had been the usual batch of customers, one was going to pop a cheque in the post, (that's always 50-50 whether I see anything) one was out, two machines un-repairable and a few successes where I actually fixed the machine and was paid. I sifted through the cheques, noticing that Maisy's was from Coutts, the London bank for the rich and famous. The days total amounted to £90 which put me just over the £509 needed to pay for my MOT. I tapped the dashboard, "All sorted, sweetheart. Now you just keep going for another year or it's over Beachy Head for an insurance claim!" I laughed to myself knowing that the 'book value' of my old girl was probably less that what it had just cost to get her through her MOT. Still, at last I had the final payment needed to hit my target. Tomorrow I would pay my outstanding bill to the garage and feel much better.

That evening while Dave and I fished for bass and mackerel we swapped stories of our day's work, laughing at all the silly adventures that make up our daily lives. The sun dropped exhausted beneath the horizon and the first welcome cool breeze of the night stroked our faces. On the far horizon storm clouds were still bubbling up. In the darkest patches we could see lightning streaking down to the sea, but it was too far away for the sound to reach us over the water.

However while we were fishing, an amazing sound did come floating over the sea. It started slowly at first but then grew and grew. Bells started to chime all along the coast, something that I had never heard before. Bells were ringing from churches all around the area and catching in the bay like an amphitheatre. Dave and I just looked at each other. I laughed and said, "Must be the end of the war." When I got home I found that, just as Maisy predicted, a new king had been born.

We caught no fish but there is always another day and that is not really what fishing is about, for most of us anyway.

Before I fell asleep that night the storm clouds rolled in and between the full moon and stars rain came down, beautiful sensuous heavy summer rain. I couldn't help thinking of Maisy who, stuffed full of rotten butter-soaked swede, would be stripping off and running around her garden in the dark looking for snails to catapult.

The next day there were two momentous events. The first was the news that flew around the world all about a special 8lb 6oz baby, born late in the afternoon the previous day, just an hour after I had left Maisy's home.

Early that evening Kate and William emerged through the double glass panelled doors of the Lindo Wing of St Mary's Hospital. They walked down the five stone steps and William came towards the press with his new son cradled in his arms. The royal baby would later to be named George Alexander Louis, but at that point, he was a prince with no name. The tiny baby had one hand raised as if he was already learning the royal wave. William introduced the new 'People's Prince' to a cheering crowd and an ever-hungry press. William looked exhausted but gloriously happy and soon returned to Kate by the steps. They waved and then disappeared inside. A new chapter in British history had begun.

Oh, I said that two important events happened that day, the second one was that I paid my car bill. I wonder which one will be noted in the history books? You gotta larf...

ANOTHER YEAR FLIES

'Blimey' I thought to myself as I drove along, 'someone's nicked another year'. It was suddenly December 2013, Christmas was nearly upon us and I still hadn't bought my wife Yana a Christmas pressie! Boy would I be in trouble. I was clearing up the last few calls before I packed away my tools for the festivities, and the idea then was to whip up to Lewes High Street to peruse all the fabulous Christmas windows and find the perfect present. Easy or what!

Thinking back, as I poodled along it seemed astonishing to me that I was still in the trade that I had been born into. Had anyone told me at school I would have laughed at them; I was going to be a millionaire and change the world, yet here I was still doing the same old job my dad had guided me into and I was still loving it. I caught a glimpse of myself in the rear-view mirror and a grey-haired old man was staring back at me. Where was that chubby-faced ball of energy? Where had all the years gone!

Once again the months had flown by at the speed of light and

2014 was knocking on the door. In years to come 2014 will seem like a long time ago but right now, as I am writing this part of my journal about life on the road, it is as far as the Human Race has got. I am at the leading edge of humanity, pulling it along in my own little way, witnessing amazing new inventions and discoveries almost on a daily basis.

I pulled off the main drag (well the A27), just past Bopeep Lane and took a right turn to Ripe. Suddenly all was quiet; I had left all the bumper to bumper traffic heading west for Brighton and beyond, and slipped into the peaceful tranquillity of a Sussex back road. The trees were winter-bare and the soaked tarmac was shining like a ribbon of black lace. Crows circled above me on the cold thermals, searching the land below for any signs of sustenance.

We'd had an easy winter so far as our Indian summer had stretched on and on. I should have guessed after the Met Office told us to prepare for the worst winter on record. The very next day the temperature rose and the wind dropped, and from then on we cruised into a warm wet winter. In spring they had predicted a wet summer and no sooner had they opened their mouths the sun came out and we had a near perfect British summer. And here we were in December with my garden fuchsias, geraniums and even a few of my roses still blooming. Along the roadsides I had also spotted marigolds. The birds were fat, scoffing all the winter berries as well as the bugs that had not died from cold, and the grass was still green. All in all it was lovely.

The first time that I heard the phrase 'global warming' I was a teenager, idly watching 'the idiot's lantern' (as my dad called

41

television), when this white-coated professor came on with a map of the world behind him. He explained the downsides, that the Earth was possibly heating up, but then went on to explain that great areas of our planet that were hostile and uninhabitable, like Greenland and Siberia, Alaska and both Poles would become warmer and humans could live in more parts of it in relative comfort. He went on to explain how England would be affected, blowing away everything that my eccentric college teacher, Latchford had drummed into us about the world entering yet another ice age. "The South of England will become more like the South of France." I paused to think of how our most famous King 'Richard The Lionheart' hated England. "It is always cold and always raining there," he moaned to his courtiers. How right he was, and in his ten year reign he spent only a few wet months here. As the professor's words sunk in I shouted "Yippee" at the television. Forty years later I am still waiting for the olive groves and vineyards.

The great news was that global warming or not, the world was cleaning up its act, which was of benefit to all mankind. Of course the bad weather would come, but each day that passed was one day closer to my favourite time of year, spring.

I shuddered when I thought back to 2012. That really was the worst year that I had ever lived through, weather wise. I remembered snow in the early 1960's and hot summers but they came and went. 2012 was harsh, bitter and seemed never-ending. Statistics told us that over 30,000 more people had died because of the extra cold alone, and then add to those all the accidents and other casualties caused by the extreme weather conditions, it was mind-boggling. It seemed amazing that if we hadn't had all our modern conveniences hardly a soul would have made it through the year.

The weather produced some amazing sights. This was a tsunami cloud roll, or horizontal tornado, over Bexhill and Eastbourne. I have never seen one before or since.

It is all so easy to forget now but the winter had shown us record gales, record cold, record winds, record snow, and record rainfall, so 2012 set all sorts of new records. We also learned new words like 'storm cells', 'sting jets', 'super cells', 'polar vortexes', and 'super storms'. We saw tornadoes sweep through Oxfordshire and cyclones with hurricane force winds rip through tiny villages. Explosive lightning storms engulfed whole towns with lightning strikes every two seconds in some areas. I watched out of my window as the Met Office announced over 3,000 strikes in two hours. Then there were the 'weather bombs', another new term to get used to. They were the strangest of all as an unexpected calm preceded them. A sudden and massive drop in pressure triggered winds of up to 140mph, which in turn slammed into towns and cities like an exploding bomb, leaving areas looking like a gang of vandals had rampaged through. As always, we tough islanders put our heads down and got on the best we could.

Out of all the natural phenomena that hit us, there were two that blew my mind, caused by ice crystals forming in the cloud layers, the technical term for one was Nacreous Clouds. It doesn't sound particularly great but when the sun rose and hit the billions of ice crystals they split the light into all the colours of the rainbow and the sky sparkled in blues and yellows, greens and reds, like some fantastic impressionist painting. The sheer scale made you stare up at the heavens in wonder. The other was Braval's Arc, an upside down rainbow that looked as if some mighty eternal being was smiling down at the world. Just like the great storm of 1987, the people who lived through the winter of 2012 in Britain, will probably talk about it for years. I know I will.

Luckily there was also our Queen's Golden Jubilee to light up the year, although even Prince Philip ended up in hospital after standing out in the rain to watch the Thames procession as over 1,000 vessels went by. Our amazing Olympics also picked us up for a few weeks, but still the awful weather continued like the ten plagues of Egypt.

Plankton was swept in from deep oceans to cover Scottish coastal

This is the Seaford to Eastbourne road as it drops down to the Cuckmere River. We don't have much snow down here but when it comes it hits hard and fast.

towns and by November the 'Beast from the East' had arrived from Siberia, bringing with it more chaos and destruction. Deep snow brought most of our roads to a standstill and hail the size of golf balls smashed down on Newcastle, ripping through conservatories and bus shelters. Vast swathes of countryside lay under flood water or snow as storm after storm hit our shuddering islands. No respite, no rest. By the end of 2012 we had witnessed the most destructive weather since records began. One day they will make documentaries and films about that foul 12 months, when Britain became nature's battleground.

The storms grew and grew over the winter and we suffered a real battering. As did Newhaven Harbour. Here the West Arm is getting a battering and all cross channel ferries were halted.

Luckily, today we are armed with better defences against nature than ever before, from central heating and double glazing to that essential survival tool, 'Cup-a-Soup'. My old Land Rover had taken me through it day by day. Over the whole of the year there were only a handful of days that we could not go out, when the roads were just shut. One day I counted 11 cars crashed just on the corner of my street alone. The good news was that more people were shut indoors and many turned to sewing, so my business had a little boost.

One morning I was driving through the snow when I came to an abrupt halt. A car had slid out of its drive and got jammed across the road, blocking all traffic. I could not understand why no one was helping the man push his car across the road until I got out of my car! As the owner was trying to move it his wife was screaming at him with all her might, calling him every name that would come to her, which she obviously overheard from a naval pub crawl. It was a hilarious scene, her leaning out of the kitchen window in her dressing gown, bright red from screaming, him cowering, his head tucked well down into his shoulders as he took an ear bashing on par with a cheap soap opera. I gathered from between the expletives that she was not too pleased that he had ignored her and tried to get to work. It was clear to me why he preferred to go to work rather than stay with his loved one! I quickly rounded up some of the other drivers and, oblivious to them, we pushed the car to the side while they continued their 'domestic'.

Comedians came up trumps as usual and Rod Gilbert had a beauty; growing up in Wales he referred to the biblical tale of Noah's Ark. "And so it rained for forty days and forty nights," he said in his thick Welsh accent and then added, "best summer we ever had."

By February of 2013 we were over the worst with one final spectacular event. Weather buoys, measuring wave height in the North Atlantic, measured a wave higher than a six storey building. At over 62ft it was the highest wave ever recorded. Following a final ferocious weather front it barrelled down from Iceland before disappearing into the unknown. An unexpected bonus was that the severe frosts turned out to be the ideal catalyst for cherry trees that went on to produce a bumper crop, so come June, I stuffed myself full of ripe home-grown Kent cherries that were being sold in bucket loads along the roadsides.

I must mention that I have a symbiotic relationship with my Land Rover. It has even got to the stage where I say 'good morning' to her each day when she sparks up. So far we have travelled the same distance as from the Earth to the Moon. The first day I picked her up Nick the salesman told me, "you are driving away the best car in the world." I often think of trying to track him down all these years later and tell him that he was right. She is a bit rusty, a bit dented and a bit rattly, but then so is her driver! Only once did I nearly lose her. There were some massive floods when she was in for repair at a body shop in Uckfield. Some crazy old man had driven straight across the Polegate Bypass without looking, smack into my path. I just managed to avoid a full frontal collision but scraped the side of my car in doing so. His excuse to the police was that he could not see what was coming so he thought he had better pull across anyway! While my baby was in for repair, the floods came.

I watched the television reports in horror as Uckfield and many other towns slowly submerged under flood water. As soon as I could I phoned the garage. "Sorry mate, all the cars have been condemned," the man on the end of the line told me. They have been bobbing about the workshop, bouncing into each other until the sewage water flooded them. Don't worry; they will be covered by insurance. 'Ang on a mo, BILL, BILL, THE DISCO..., IT'S KNACKERED, AIN'T IT?" I waited in silence, fearing the worst. He came back on the phone, "Your lucky day mate. The Disco was one of only two cars up on the ramps. Dry as a bone, untouched. I'll let you know when she is ready for collection." So my baby was saved and back on the road we went, through thick and thin, rain and snow. Together we ply our trade across Sussex and earn our living.

I once met an old farmer who had a tractor that he had used for over 40 years. He said to me that he loved his tractor and he loved his wife but he knew which one he could not do without. Bad boy!

I was still trying to decide what I should buy my darling wife for Christmas as the barriers dropped at the Chalvington railway crossing, on my way to the first call of the morning. Over the other side of the line a farmer was ploughing up a grain field and a thousand gulls chased the tractor, diving for fresh worms and grubs. I looked along the rail tracks in the direction of Lewes, and just above the railway line was an enormous full moon, so clear and crisp it looked like it had sunken down to Lewes to pop in for a coffee. I could almost see the lunar rover that the Chinese had just landed there called Jade Rabbit. I glanced to my right and on the lea side of the Downs, just along from the Long Man Giant at Wilmington, the sun was rising over the fields. It was in its early soft orange mode, moving majestically upward as the moon dropped down. For a moment they looked directly at each other along the shining railway line, two immortals, face to face in the first morning light. I was twisting my head from one to the other in disbelief. All I needed was a camera that took a picture from both sides.

I was fully entranced when the railway line started its familiar whistling whine that signalled the London train was nearing. It rushed by at full speed, buffeting the trees as it rocketed its passengers to Eastbourne. The bleeping barriers rose and I took a last look at the majestic giants before bumping over the tracks on my way to Langtye Farmhouse. Hilary had originally found my phone number from a 'Stitch & Bitch' meeting at her local village hall. It always made me laugh when I heard that term (which even the posh women seem to enjoy using).

I parked up and made my way to the back of the Disco to pull out my toolbox. I heard a roar coming along the lane and spotted a huge Toyota Land Cruiser gobbling up the road with alarming speed. I made it to the side of my car just as the driver shot by, spraying me with water. The woman driver was applying lipstick and both kids in the back had their noses tucked into some computer games. I doubt if she even saw me. I just shook my head in disbelief, but in reality I had seen crazy driving along country lanes a thousand times.

As I opened the gate to Hilary's farmhouse I scared away a handful of pheasants that had escaped from 'shoots' at the Firle Estates. "I have named them all, Alex," came a voice from the front door. "That beauty is Ebenezer and he has at least three wives," said Hilary as she pointed at a brightly coloured pheasant. He stopped on the back wall to look at me and decide if I had a gun or not, but he soon returned to the bird table to continue pecking at the scraps.

After servicing Hilary's 21st birthday present I hit the road and headed for the ancient Viking settlement of Laughton, 'The Home of the Buckle'. People think that Laughton must have been instrumental in the manufacture and supply of belt and shoe buckles, all centred around the now sleepy village, but that is not the case.

The village actually came by its unusual nickname because of Sir John Pelham. I was lucky enough to bump into a local historian many years ago who lived behind the village shop. Outside her door were piles of eggs for sale and inside was a fount of all knowledge about Laughton. Betsy was such a funny girl, a perfect copy of the lady of the manor but with no money and loads of attitude. When I asked a silly question, she stopped and looked down her nose at me, then asked where I was born. I told her Eastbourne and she nodded knowingly, then spouted out, "Ah I see, a Sussex lad born and bred, strong in the arm but weak in the head." We both burst out laughing. I knew she was just kidding, well I hoped she was!

As I slowly worked through her sewing machine, she filled me in on the historic link of Laughton, the buckle, and the once famous Pelham family. It is a cracker of a tale.

The Pelhams of Laughton could trace their ancestors back to before the Domesday Book and for almost as long, their history has been entwined with royalty. At one time their lands stretched across vast parts of Southern England, from Chichester to Rye. The Pelhams (who held the title of the Earls of Chichester) did so much for the churches around my area that many of the towers became known as 'Pelham Towers'. All the church towers had one thing in common, they all displayed versions of a buckle (depending on the stone mason's carving) with the buckle point always upwards. Ashburnham, Chalvington, Chiddingly, Crowhurst, Dallington, East Hoathly, Laughton, Ripe, Waldron and a few that I have probably missed are all supposed to display the Pelham Buckle. So now that I have made you so curious I will explain how this once powerful family came to have a buckle on its heraldic family crest.

There are several local legends about the Pelham family but the most glorious one was set during the 100 Years War between France and England, and is possibly the legend that made Laughton 'the home of the buckle'. There were many battles in France during that period and in 1356 the French king had decided enough was enough. Edward, The Black Prince was up to no good again, raiding lands in France and burning towns and villages along the way. As he fled back to his stronghold in Aquitaine (with all his goodies) he left behind him a scorched earth policy for which he had become notorious.

The Black Prince (Edward of Woodstock) was the eldest son of King Edward III and no one is positive why he had this nickname. Some say it was given to him by his French opponents because of the shining black armour that he wore in battle, others that it was because his mother Philippa was of Moorish descent. Some say that he earned it from his terrible deeds that were as black as pitch.

The Black Prince had a short and violent life and during one of his destructive raids King Jean II managed to trap Edward's army at Poitiers. Unfortunately for the French King it all went terribly wrong when he came up against the fearless warrior and his skilled and seasoned fighters.

As the fighting raged at the famous Battle of Poitiers, King Jean found himself surrounded and outmanoeuvred. He was fighting with his 14 year old son by his side, and what should have been a glorious victory for his son to behold turned into a desperate fight to the death. However, in crashes Sir John Pelham and Sir Roger de la Warr, who (along with their soldiers) offered King

Jean protection if he yielded. The king sheathed his sword, removed his helmet and surrendered to Pelham and de la Warr. The banners were lowered and the battle won. By the time Edward Prince of Wales rode over, Pelham had been handed King Jean's sword and belt, complete with the fancy royal buckle. A great feast was later held to celebrate a momentous English victory and another legend for The Black Prince was born. The French King was later ransomed for a fortune.

Both Sir John and Sir Roger were honoured for their exploits by King Edward III. Sir Roger (for his lesser part) was given the French King's gold crampet (a small metal part of the scabbard), and Sir John was given the French King's impressive buckle to keep as a badge of honour, to be worn and shown with pride. From that point in history both families used these honours to decorate their family crests and the Battle of Poitiers entered the history books forever.

Back home in England, in 1401, the wealthy Pelham family leased the Manor of Laughton from the De Vere Family and in 1466 the Pelham Family bought much of Laughton for 1,000 marks. The old moated manor at Laughton became their main home and the Pelham name part of the local folklore.

Unfortunately, as with so many powerful old families, crippling death duties after The Second World War forced The Earl of Chichester to liquidate many of his holdings. The last connection with Laughton was sold off in the 1960's and the family's historic link with the village faded into local legend.

Laughton Church is one of the few places left that you can still find the Laughton Buckle. Inside and around the picturesque flint church there are some surprisingly important historical figures buried.

If you ever get the chance to pop into the beautiful All Saint's Church in Laughton you will find the Pelham family vault, where many Pelhams are laid to rest (the serving priests paid to chant for their souls). The church is surprisingly plain inside for an ancient monument dating right back to the 13th century. The Pelham Vault is beneath the chancel, covered with an old carpet. Down there are some of the great men of history including The Duke of Newcastle, Thomas Pelham Holles (a protégé of Sir

Here is a Laughton Buckle made famous by the Pelham Family and the Battle of Poitiers.

Robert Walpole) and his brother Henry, both of whom served time as Prime Minister. There are also at least three Earls of Chichester, and George Pelham who was Bishop of Bristol, Exeter and finally Lincoln. Over thirty Pelhams are interred in the family vault, its entrance sealed to stop vandals. Some of the great and the powerful men of history who once shaped the path of our nation, are silently resting beneath that worn carpet in the sleepy village church.

There is a great example of 'The Buckle' on Coldharbour Farmhouse, down Whitesmith Lane. Or if you feel confident enough, you could knock on Jill's door opposite the church in Laughton, as she has a beautifully carved copy of the buckle in her garden. And so that is how Laughton became the home of the buckle, but before we leave the church I must mention another tomb and the legend that goes with it.

Near the churchyard gate is a large red granite tomb. In the tomb is both Sir James Duke and his son. Sir James bought Laughton Lodge and built many properties in the village. He was a distinguished Member of Parliament and became Lord Mayor of London in 1848. The village tale tells that if you wait near the tomb till midnight on All Hallows' Eve, then hold your breath and walk around the tomb anticlockwise three times without a breath, the devil will appear and grant you a wish!

Don't you just love these weird bits of English history that dot our landscape, almost as plentiful as the sheep that graze it?

Carrying on with my calls, by the time I neared Laughton Village the sun was up and the moon had dropped below the horizon. The brilliant light was reflecting back from the electricity pylons towards Ringmer, lighting them up in a blaze of steely orange. In the far distance I could see the Glynde wind turbine scooping up air as it caught the fresh sea breeze rushing up the valley.

My old girl grappled her way along the lumpy back roads, in and out of the puddles, throwing up great sloshes of muddy water over the verges and ditches as she went. I rode along in dry comfort thinking how, in all of history, just my short journey would have been hard and harsh. Now I was sliding along in comfort and warmth, knowing that my next customer in Church Lane would probably have the kettle on. She had kept a parking spot for me because, at that time of day, the road often became clogged with mothers dropping their kids off at the school by the church. Sure enough as I neared I spotted two red traffic cones outside her house. I smiled in approval and slipped into the space provided. I spotted a crest embossed in stone above her door frame and knew instantly that, like so many buildings in the area, it once belonged to the Pelham estates.

I grabbed my tools out of the back of the Land Rover, slammed the door shut with a deft swing of my hips and walked to one of my last customers of 2013, whistling as I went. Another of my daily visits was under way, visits that I had carried out week after week, year after year. I turned to see my old girl steaming in the morning light and dripping as if she had just climbed out of the shower. Sure enough that Land Rover loves her job as much as I do. I almost waved to her but I stopped myself just in time as a bunch of noisy mothers cackled by. No need to get certified just before Christmas!

By late morning I parked in Lewes, down by the brewery, jumped out of my car and caught my breath as a cold breeze swept up my nostrils. It was full of Harvey's malt ale. One of the wonders of Lewes is its brilliant brewery smell that often sits in the folds of the low lying areas at the bottom of the hill. I walked up the twitten that cuts to the main shops and came out near the river. I looked up the busy road where people were rushing here

Sometimes getting to work was tricky as so many roads were flooded. Here is Lewes at the height of the floods during the winter of 2013-14. Luckily my old banger can almost swim. Several times I was suddenly driving through flooded country lanes trying to reach my customers.

and there in a pre-Christmas shopping frenzy and a cold shudder went down my spine. I had a pocket full of money and absolutely no idea what to buy Yana. It suddenly dawned on me the enormity of my predicament. I could see the high street stretching up the hill to the law courts and in my mind's eye I could visualise most of the shops where I might find something suitable; White Stuff Fashions perhaps?

Sweet Mary mother of Jesus, what on earth to do next. Panic started to set in. Like many men I hate shopping and had put off the fateful day for way too long. Now there was no time left. I headed for the closest coffee shop to stock up on sustenance and make a good plan, for as every good husband knows, my very life probably depended on the next move.

THE END

Lewes Castle sits above Lewes like a current on a bun. It is a steep climb but from the top of the battlements you get one of the finest views in the area.

MIDNIGHT CALLER

Death's a come a knocking,
A knocking on my door.
He's passed by a few times,
But never stopped before.

Should I let him in?
Have I got a choice?
He seems a friendly fellow,
With that deep mellow voice.

Now the door is open,
I manage a weak croak.
"Do enter my dear chap."
"The maid will take your cloak."

Soon he's by the fire,
Looking quite the cock,
He says he knows my family,
Which comes as quite a shock.

Of course it all makes sense
He's met them all you see,
Those long lost rellies,
From my family tree.

I dare not ask the reason,
For his midnight call.
But drink gives me courage,
"Am I heading for a fall?"

"Oh no," he whispers lightly,
"You have a year or two,
I saw your light a shining,
And thought I'd visit you."

"It's old Ada round the corner,
You know, she's done her best.
She's ninety four and counting,
And it's time for her to rest."

"So I've a come a knocking,
An unexpected call,
To wish you season's greetings.
Merry Christmas one and all."

A I A

On The Road Again

The fields were covered with corpses and all around the
only colour to meet the gaze was blood red. It looked
from afar as if rivulets of blood, flowing down from all
sides, had filled the valleys.
Chronicles of Battle Abbey, 1180

It was 7.30 in the morning and I was standing in Heathfield
Market, staring at a trader who must have modelled himself on
Flash Harry straight out of an old St Trinian's film. "Can't take
less than a ton for it," said Flash with a shrug. He was wearing
an enormous black Cromby coat with padded shoulders, his head
was tucked down into his coat and he was taking shifty glances
left and right. I was half expecting him to swing open his coat and
show me a row of counterfeit watches. "Well, sixty is my limit,"
I told him in a firm voice, "but it's cash and I'll take it with me
now." I glanced away with a bored look as if it didn't matter, but
in his possession he had a beautiful old Singer that I would just
love to add to my collection. "Done" said Flash with a nod. I
quickly parted with my hard earned money, thinking that I was
glad that he hadn't spat into the palm of his hand to seal the deal

with a slimy shake. Flash licked his index finger and counted the notes. The money disappeared into an inner pocket like a magician's rabbit and he passed me the machine that had been stuffed between his feet. As soon as I got hold of it he pulled his collar up and went. "'Ave a good one" he shouted back to me, as he disappeared into the market crowd.

I smiled to myself and put the machine carefully into my car. Heathfield Market has always been a good hunting ground for old sewing machines. Time to get to work, I thought. I could play with my new acquisition later. I hit the road to my first call of the day, which was at a convent just off the High Street in Uckfield.

If all my calls went well, by the end of the day I would be standing at Standard Hill near Ninfield with money in my pocket and a handful of happy customers. That's if all went well! I had learnt through hard experience that if there is a spanner to be thrown into the works it would be; it's called Sod's Law or really it is just life, depending on your point of view. Over the years I have perfected the ability to catch some of the flying spanners that are thrown my way and add them to my toolbox rather than let the day fall apart. I always try to be prepared for anything from car crashes to breakdowns, bad customers, flat tyres and even worse sewing machines. If I have one motto it is, 'try and be prepared'. The thousands of parts that I carry in the back of my car prove my point. Each time I find the part I need from my spares it feels like a little pat on the back for being prepared.

My working day had started well and I was aiming for a busy few hours, with a tank full of fuel and a load of regulars to call on.

Before long I was working my way through the nuns' sewing machines in Uckfield. I smiled as they fussed around me like a whirlwind of bats when suddenly a searing pain shot across my chest. I stopped instantly, thinking 'I didn't like the feel of that'. Then another, this time across my chest and up the left side of my neck. As the third electric pain shot across my body, up my neck and down my left arm I knew it was a heart attack. I had suffered with heart problems since my late 20's so it was no big surprise. I stood up, and while all those around me were totally unaware of my pain, I reviewed my circumstances. A good place to die I thought! Surrounded by nuns. I was sure to get a first class ticket to meet St Peter, and an access all areas pass into heaven.

I was chubby (relaxed muscle of course), on medication and the perfect age for a nice coronary. At 56, by any bygone standards of life I would have been the old man in the village with my days numbered. In biblical times, if you were pure of spirit and obeyed the Ten Commandments, the good Lord might bless you with three score years and ten but precious few would ever reach that staggering age. Today we have a different view on age and 70 doesn't seem so old anymore.

I stretched my neck and sat down, waiting for the big one but it didn't come. I realised that my breathing was slow and deep, just the opposite of a heart attack and the pains were outside my ribs not deep inside. I'm going to live, I thought, no Reaper today.

When we are young we do battle with the world, but when we get older we wage a battle against ourselves and our own bodies, often in a losing bid to drag out more precious time on earth. Aren't we so surprised to find out that we are mortal! Some people rage against the injustice of a surprise attack from within, others scream until their brains overload in anger and many just fade away. We humans still have so much to learn. I, on the other hand, had thousands of wise old dears who regularly showered their pearly wisdom over me like fresh rain. When my eyes started to go and I struggled with my new glasses my customers would laugh. "Eyes, that's the least of your worries," they would tell me. "Take the pills and toughen up," seemed to be the general consensus from most of them; being old is no place for the weak!

Examining what I thought had been my last moments of life I had no regrets, no flashing images rushed before my eyes; I was calm and prepared. Sister Mary came in with a cup of tea propped up with two digestives. Yippee, miracle food for sure. I suddenly remembered that I had been pruning trees in my garden the day before, swinging like a fat monkey in the branches. I had probably just strained a few muscles. I had done it many times before with similar effects the following day.

"You look a bit concerned, Alex?" said Mary as she put the tray down next to me.

"I thought I was having a heart attack."

"You daft sod," she laughed before whispering, "Forgive me Lord." Mary went on to explain that she had been a cardiac nurse for 34 years and I didn't have that awful grey pallor or shortness of breath. "In fact you look as healthy as a farmer's prize bull. You will probably outlive us all. Now you have a nice cup of tea, nothing revives the soul like a nice cuppa."

With the tea swallowed and the biscuits munched, I finished off servicing the sewing machines. I brushed the crumbs from my trousers, took a few token blessings from the grateful convent

Pure delight, tea and treats at the convent.

girls and hit the road with renewed zest, this time for a farm near Burwash. I swallowed an aspirin as well, just to be on the safe side! As I was driving, Willie Nelson came on the radio and started singing in his gravelly tones 'On The Road Again', how perfect I thought as I trundled along. I am on the road again, still alive and still rocking.

At Burwash I found Farmer Dick wrapping old sheep skins around the base of his fruit trees. He told me how they protected the roots, kept in moisture during the dry season and fertilised the soil as they slowly rotted away. As an added bonus they also provided the perfect nesting materials for his prized kingfishers that lived down by his stream.

As I walked into my next call at Burwash Village Hall, I was delighted to see a brand new resuscitation unit bolted to the wall. The old regulars at the hall knew exactly what to do when one of their colleagues bit the dust halfway through a recital of the Mikado or some Christmas panto.

I was visiting the Burwash Sewing Girls to test their sewing machines with an electrical 'Portable Appliance' or PAT tester. Some insurance companies had found a great 'get out of jail free card' by adding small print into their complicated legal packs, stating that all portable machinery being brought into their buildings must be regularly tested for electrical safety, which of course many people have missed, to their peril. The Burwash Girls however had spotted it and called me in to test each sewing machine for electrical safety. It was a quick job and as I looked around the large sewing table I realised that I had called on every single woman to repair their sewing machines at one time or another. As I left I shouted goodbye and like a church choir they sung in unison, "Goodbye Alex." Everyone laughed and I smiled. Daylight was burning and I had many miles to go before my last call at Standard Hill near Ninfield.

My next call was at Hurst Green, a few miles north of Battle, where a rare old Elna hand sewing machine was awaiting my attention. I drove along the winding road from Burwash past Etchingham, noting a new café in the railway station for later perusal. I went by the Burgh Hill turning on my left, twisting up the winding road of Haremere Hill. On the right was a small track, easily missed, which I knew led to a fascinating building that is still making news many centuries after it was made. It is called Haremere Hall, and they say that it is haunted! You can

Some say the impressive Jacobean house, Haremere Hall, is haunted by the ghost of John Busbridge.

rent it for a mere £2,000-a-week, if you dare. Like so many of our local grand houses it is packed with history and tales that would keep a storyteller happy for years. Only locals and people who have stayed there even know that it exists as it is tucked away so perfectly, just out of eyesight off the main highway.

The Grade I listed country manor is a sight to behold. It looks like it is trapped in a time warp amongst the ancient folds of the Sussex countryside; the Jacobean jewel is one of the many hidden treasures of my area. Locals tell that the present house, built around 1616 was built on foundations dating back to 1066, after William Duke of Normandy passed out parcels of land to his faithful warriors.

During the English Civil War the house owner, royalist John

Busbridge, was leaning out of a window, negotiating with Cromwellian soldiers when a sniper shot him dead. Some say that it is his ghost who haunts the place on dark windy nights. The previous owner who had lost the property to Busbridge was probably behind the shooting but no proof was ever forwarded. He was James Temple, one of Cromwell's cronies and one of the 59 judges who later passed the death sentence on King Charles I. He rose to prominence under Cromwell but after the Restoration he was a man on the run. He was later caught and convicted of the unusual crime of 'king killing' or regicide, but after forfeiting most of his wealth and all of his lands he was allowed to escape the gallows. Instead he was imprisoned until his death in a jail on Jersey.

Over the years the house seems to have had one grand owner after another and early in the 19th century, Sir John Lade was in residence. He was a fine horseman, a close friend of King George IV and one of Samuel Johnson's gambling buddies. His talents lay in spotting great horse flesh and losing chunks of his wealth on impetuous bets. Blimey, how the other half live eh? In that age everyone of importance seemed to know him as he was easily spotted, often dressed in colourful riding garb and carrying a riding whip with him, even in the centre of London. Apparently his wife had the reputation of being a woman of 'loose character', wasting much of Lade's vast brewing inheritance whilst having dalliances with other men, including allegedly, the Duke of York.

And so the impressive manor carried on sheltering these colourful characters, one after the other until along came Lady Killearn whose husband, Baron Killearn, bought the hall after

The Second World War. Even today Lady Killearn is still 'making the papers' at the tender age of 104, and for all the wrong reasons. Lady Killearn lived in style and rose to the pinnacle of high society, entertaining royalty and aristocracy alike from King Farouk of Egypt to Winston Churchill, who lived just up the road at Chartwell. She was from a forgotten world and tried to live in the style of the Old Empire, whose glory days had long since faded. Even Charles de Gaulle, the most famous Frenchman since Napoleon was entertained at her pleasure.

However, Britain's oldest socialite had fallen out with her son and heir. Lady Jackie Killearn had tried to sell off her son's Jacobean inheritance at a knock-down price for a quick sale. Her son Victor (Lord Killearn), had stepped in and it all ended up in court. I can just see the solicitors' faces when four years earlier they were instructed to take the 100yr old mother to court! Haremere Hall was held in a family trust, but Lady Killearn wanted money for her other London properties and decided, much to the annoyance of her son, to flog the old manor for whatever she could get.

While writing this, she had just been to the High Court to try and overturn an earlier ruling in her son's favour to stop her selling the property. She still owns, amongst other places, a huge property in Harley Street, London and Bickleigh Castle in Devon, so she is not too hard up for a place to stay. Although she rents out Haremere Hall to holiday-makers, apparently there are always apartments kept there for the family so that they can stay.

Lady Killearn is a fascinating figure, she even fell out with her butler who, according to his accounts, after too much abuse finally took her to court for unfair dismissal. He was paid compensation for having to suffer her outbursts and flying walking sticks! All in all she is brilliant for gossip and a colourful character that has kept the tabloids entertained these many years.

I thought to myself that I must whip down the lane and get a photo of the splendid but dilapidated old Jacobean manor, just in case some rich Russian oligarch snaps it up and slaps security all over it. Then one of our Sussex jewels will be hidden away for years only to be resurrected at some later point in history, with even more fascinating tales attached.

I carried on to my call in Hurst Green and sitting on a table waiting patiently for attention was the sweet old Elna. While I was fixing it I couldn't help thinking that you may have all the power and wealth in the world but that elusive little thing called happiness is another story entirely.

From Hurst Green it was up to Ticehurst and Tinker's lane, near Three Legged Cross where Liz was waiting. Liz had a big old machine for her horse rugs and it often went out of kilter. The hours slipped away and before long I was rolling homeward with just the final call left at Standard Hill. It had been a good day, all had gone well and I even managed a cup of coffee and a sandwich at Bewl Reservoir. There had been no spanners in the works today.

As I dropped down to Battle I caught glimpses of the coastline; the area from Ticehurst down to Ninfield has to be one of the most beautiful in the world. Pretty chocolate box villages and teashops, country churches, old manors and farms all dotted into a timeless landscape of wooded countryside, stretching out mile after mile. If ever you have a spare hour or two, come to the ancient land of the South Saxons and drive around the villages on the Sussex-Kent borders. On the right day you will find a patch of heaven.

When I walked in on my last customer she was squeezing out an impressive and ear-bending rendition of Amazing Grace on her bagpipes. If ever there was a tune for a funeral that was it. I don't mean that in a bad way, Amazing Grace goes straight to the heart. It might be because of the person who wrote it, and the anguish he felt as he penned the words. John Newton was a slave trader who turned to God and later wrote the words to Amazing Grace. The tune was added and immortality followed. I say immortality because I'm sure that as long as humans are on this earth, Amazing Grace will be played.

I fixed my final machine of the day, packed up my tools and walked to my car from where I could clearly see the high lands around Battle. I stopped for a moment and tried to soak in the importance of where I stood. Today it is all calm and peaceful, pretty gardens and sweet country lanes, but for a short time in 1066 this was the most important place in the known world. If you stand very quiet at Standard Hill you can feel the very presence of history oozing out of the ground.

Standard Hill is where legend tells us William Duke of Normandy put up his banners, flags and standards the night before he changed English history in 1066. A few miles north on higher ground, Harold was set up at Lovers Lane along Caldbec Hill, just above what we now call Battle. He thought his stunning stomp across England had caught William by surprise. How wrong he was.

The night before the bloody conflict, men from either sides prayed to their priests for forgiveness of their many sins (so that if killed they could enter heaven pure of spirit). Whatever the experts tell us today, back in October of 1066 the fires from both camps would have been clearly visible in the darkness. The following day William moved up the high road from Ninfield, joined with more of his men coming up the ancient Hastings Road, and set out toward Harold and his troops who were already waiting at the ridge of the hill.

William had played 'the long game' and history tells us that it was probably his sneaky dealings that led to the Viking attack up north. You have to remember that all parties fighting for control of England were of Viking descent and the Battle of Hastings was really the climax of the Viking wars, leaving one man standing.

Harold's stunning victory at Stamford Bridge just days earlier had left his army severely depleted. Harold had rushed back across the country in a forced stomp that still has historians talking about it in glorious terms, but it was a huge mistake. Harold left behind most of his archers and if there was one deciding factor in the battle it was that. Harold was expecting William to make for London so his mad dash across the country to save the city made sense but William had outsmarted him again.

William stayed in sight of supplies and ships, harrying the area around Pevensey and Hastings, basically poking the wounded bear. This was to lure Harold into his trap. William might have been poking the bear but he also had the strength to kill it. He brought to England cutting edge technology and techniques, which he had perfected, while fighting for power in Europe (since taking over from his father at eight years old). The Saxons would find this out to their cost. As well as his superior archers, highly paid mercenaries and crossbowmen he had a superb mounted cavalry, not seen since Roman times. The horsemen not only had amazing weaponry, spears, lances, slashing swords and more, they had better saddles with straps and stirrups and superior protection. The Saxons had never faced a mounted cavalry charge on trained heavy horse. This, combined with William's archers would spell the end of Saxon rule in our country leaving just the ancient name of Sussex to remember them by.

Harold's early start had blocked William's path at the narrowing on a ridge, where a local landmark, an old grey twisted apple tree hung over the London road. Today the spot is marked by a mini roundabout where Marley Lane joins the Battle road, just to the east of Battle Abbey.

He spread his men along the ridge in what he thought would be an impenetrable wall of death. The Saxon Shield Wall had never broken on an uphill charge. Harold had thought he had stolen a march on William, just like he had done when he surprised the Viking Army at Stamford. However, William knew exactly where he wanted to fight and what he wanted to do.

He needed a large open range where his horsemen could destroy the Saxons and his archers had a clear field of view. Specially trained archers from Louviers and Evreux used their traditional short bows, well developed from their Viking hunting heritage, but with a subtle and deadly improvement, they used a combination of short and long arrowheads or bodkins. The longer bodkins could pierce chainmail and the shorter ones could fly high in the air, covering nearly 300 yards with a following wind.

All William had to do was lure them into his ambush, close the trap and unleash his arrow-storm, which as we all know, he did

The Bayeux Tapestry was probably commissioned by Bishop Odo (Bishop of Bayeux), the half-brother of William the Conqueror. Odo was in the thick of the fighting at The Battle of Hastings and in the final attack, so the tapestry could be a reasonable version of events. Harold is surrounded by Norman archers (who held high status amongst their army unlike the Saxons who considered their archers as low rank). You can clearly see the last stand of Harold, (his brothers already dead), his remaining few men surrounding him, their shields full of holes and peppered with arrows. Even as Harold succumbs to an arrow in the eye (and then finished off by horsemen) you can see the other Normans stripping the dead Saxons of their weapons and clothing. Odo went on to become one of the most powerful men in England, known as The Tyrannical Earl of Kent.

with ruthless efficiency. Throughout the day he picked off men with sustained archery volleys and fake charges and when Harold's men eventually fell for his ploy, (probably due to frustration as much as anything) his mounted killers went to work, trampling and destroying wave after wave of Saxon men.

Late in the afternoon, Harold, (who had been King of England for only one violent year) and his remaining men, were holding the last of the high ground. They formed their shield walls and stood shoulder to shoulder against the invaders who were now moving uphill in force. The Normans (re-supplied with more arrows from Crowhurst) were firing two volleys of arrows simultaneously, the first high into the sky the second just above ground level. The weakened Saxon shield wall, now in limited numbers, could only protect high or low, not both. This devastating method was to prove the final undoing for our ruler and his knights.

It was on the ridge that Harold made a last desperate attempt to stop the foreign usurper who had laid waste to his family's lands along the coast, but he had been coaxed into a steel trap with no hope of escape. It was here that the old Saxon war machine met a modern European army that, outnumbered, fighting on unfamiliar ground and uphill used their new technologies to blow away the old order and replace it with a new ruling dynasty. One bloody day that changed our world forever.

Arrows make a whistling whoosh as they fly and amongst the screams and thunder of that final surge it is said that Harold was hit in the eye with a Norman light-bodkin arrow coming out of the lowering sun. In that second the outcome of the battle was decided. As Harold, Earl of Wessex, the last Anglo-Saxon king of England lay dying, his men, the men of the sea axe, the Saxons, were crushed forever. The time of the Normans had begun.

Amazingly not one single artefact, skeleton, arrowhead or piece of armour has ever been found at Battle. Even when Time Team used all their technologies they came up with nothing, except that the plaque marking the spot where Harold fell was in the wrong place and needed moving! The only possible clue was dug up in a garden down Marley Lane in the 1950's. It is a rusty lump of metal that may have been an axe head and is now in Battle Museum. One day forensics will tell us if it had been used on that fateful day in the autumn of 1066.

The events of that day in 1066 cast a long shadow and centuries later, Battle Abbey, built in homage to God for William's glorious victory on Senlac Field, was taken over by Henry VIII as part of

I once found a metal artefact near Battle while searching for one of my arrows in an archery field. I was so excited, immediately assuming that I had discovered the only artefact ever found from the famous battle. After testing it turned out to be a molten blob from a metal can! Oh well.

his Dissolution of the Monasteries. He raised huge monies from his 'church sales' and used much of it to build fortifications all along the coasts of England. These castles were built by selling the wealth of the Roman Catholic Church. The fortifications were in turn to protect the new religion that he and his lover, Anne Boleyn had started. Little good it did her!

Henry then gave the Abbey to his Master of Horse, Sir Anthony Browne who converted the Abbey into a private house. Today it

Battle Abbey is amazing with a large amount of buildings set over many acres of land, from the visitors centre and ruined abbey buildings, to a great tea room and even a school.

is part school and part Visitors Centre for English Heritage, plus a great place for a sandwich and coffee. They also have brilliant audio tours of parts of the battlefield, which gives a taste of the fury and fear that must have erupted there so long ago.

I often smile to myself when I bump over the mini roundabout at the Marley Lane and Hastings Road junction. The roundabout is at the very centre of where much of the action took place on that momentous day, but those great events are now hidden under tarmac and brick. Nearly all traces of that explosive day, when England shuddered are gone. They are hidden by houses and shops lining the roadside that cater for the endless stream of tourists visiting Battle. Little do the visitors realise, when sipping their lattes and buying their touristy knick-knacks in the many shops, that they are actually standing where much of the most ferocious action took place almost a thousand years ago. Amazing, simply amazing.

Heart pumping stuff, I thought to myself as I took a deep breath and jumped into my old banger. She sparked into life and I pointed her towards home. I suddenly remembered the old Singer I had bought that morning from 'Flash'. It seemed like another lifetime ago but in reality just a few short hours had passed since I was standing in that windy market doing some horse trading. I knew that I would be drooling over the machine in my garage after supper.

Another day driving through the history and lanes of my beloved Sussex was coming to a close. Sweet mother superior, I thought as I rumbled down the Wartling road, I must have the best job ever.

POST SCRIPT
As I had finished this piece in May of 2015, I found out that Lady Killearn (who was 105 in January of 2015), had, against all odds

and legal challenges, managed to sell Haremere Hall and 100 acres of heaven for just over £2 million. The gates were closed and all access to the little Sussex jewel has been lost. I bet her son, the current Lord Killearn, (who tried everything he could to keep hold of his family pile) is just about as furious as he can be. He's probably still sizzling!

THE END

This is how I spend many of my evenings after buying an old relic that needs rebuilding. I love working on the Myford ML7 lathe, making a part for a machine. Working on an old lathe is more intuitive engineering, done by feel and sound, rather than the computer operated CNC machines of today.

I don't normally write books about one person but with Norman and Isaac Singer their tales were just too amazing so they had to have their own books.

As book sales have flourished our local postman Dan Stirrups made an extra effort to collect the copies for posting all over the world. My book on Isaac Singer went straight in as the No1 New release on Amazon. I didn't last long but I had a smile as big as the Cheshire Cat for a month. Luckily, my publishers in America and here in the UK let me have plenty of copies for my friends. Now all I need is a nice library.

Fishing has been a lifelong hobby of mine since my dad jumbled us all into the back of his car and dropped us at the seafront for the day. It must be the hunter gatherer instinct still coming out of me, even though I don't keep many of the fish these days. They say that a bad day fishing is better than a good day at work. I have worked out that one hour at work needs three hours fishing to undo the knots.

I have spent a lifetime collecting some of the finest 19th Century sewing machines ever made. I spend hours getting each machine working and on my Sewalot Site I include their history and the pioneers that designed and made them.

The row of machines are Civil War era machines made in America and Canada.

The Dolly Varden is the only sewing machine that I have ever come across named after a character created by Charles Dickens. His descriptions in Barnaby Rudge were so good that the Dolly Varden fashion craze swept the world. It is said that Dickens had a portrait of the fictitious Dolly above his desk until the day he died.

The great thing about my trade is that I get to see and work with some superb fabrics, from the finest silks costing thousands to the best leathers. I even get to take some home for my projects.

I never really know what the day will bring; one moment I will be working at a school with a row of damaged sewing machines, the next working on a fully computerised 15-needle embroidery machine that needs rebuilding then reprograming. I could say that it's all in a day's work but the SWF embroidery machine took me two days to fix! I can laugh now but I quoted £65 for the repair and stuck to it.

February

Days now drag with feet of lead,
And bitter winds rule the roost.
We dream of the warmth ahead,
To give our hearts a small boost.

We watch the birds preparing,
For they know what's round the bend.
With their songs they are sharing,
A glimpse of the winter's end.

A I A

SPRING

It was the first day of spring 2014 and what a day! The heavy rain that had fallen for days was suddenly swept away by a cool westerly, leaving just the most perfect pristine blue skies. The wettest winter on record had finally disappeared into the memory banks, for old people to chat about on street corners and around coffee tables. The papers had a field day of course, showing photos of the flooding, plus a few enhanced pictures like the surfers surfing up Bude High Street (which turned out not to be the High Street at all but the river close by).

The Somerset Levels suffered their highest rainfall on record and 25 square miles of farmland was submerged under the deluge. Luckily the low lying land was used to flooding and the largest pumping operation in modern history was quickly mobilised. Nearly nine million tonnes of water a day was pumped back into the rivers which flowed into the Bristol Channel.

However, as March 21st arrived our annual rebirth was in full swing; daffodils danced and cherry trees bloomed. The sea that had churned and boiled like a steaming fury in a witches cauldron for most of the winter had become calm and serene. She was resting, recovering, at peace, and looked like a satin sheet of the finest silk rippled over an enormous bed. Our local vicar had a bounce in his step and joyous words for all.

It always takes me by surprise just how quickly our world wakes up after winter. One moment the trees seem barren of all life as their grey branches howl in the bitter wind, the next a hint of green, no more than a smudge and then bang! Our brief British spring arrives with such promise; we turn our faces to the warm sun and dream of the great days ahead. Everyone loves spring, don't you, of course you do! Funnily I can tell the turning of the winter season by a modern marvel, my solar lights.

My garden is crammed with solar lights following my spotty teenager fascination with electrics at college. I was obsessed with using power from our sun, so many millions of miles away. It seemed almost magical that these new-fangled solar panels could work using power from the cosmos. I had rows of silly switches and contraptions on my window sill that would react in the most basic way to our free energy. Now technology has raced forward and I have plastered my garden with these 'night delights'. It is to my embarrassment and utter delight that my garden has become known by friends and neighbours as 'Little Blackpool'.

The solar lights had been dark for weeks but during the second week of February I noticed that three of them had come on. It meant that the sun was rising slightly higher in the sky. Within weeks every working light was glowing after dark and by the spring equinox in March, the garden was a blaze of colour every night. Of course the plants and trees know the changing seasons and send out tiny leaves like advance search parties. If they meet with success more follow and in a heartbeat the beautiful rainbow colours of spring dance in our gardens and hedgerows. In March the whole of Sussex turns into a blaze of colours, prettier than a Persian prayer mat with views that blow kisses to your heart.

It was Friday morning, I was on a mission to get to Bexhill and Norman's superb haberdashery shop in St Leonards Road called Thimble-Inas (a play on the words of the old fairy tale). I had to be at his shop by 11.00am as one of his regular customers was hiring a taxi to take her sewing machine in and I had to fix it for her as quickly as possible while she waited.

As I drove along the old Normans Bay road to my first call of the morning I could see the farmer along the flatlands patrolling his fields. He was looking for any of his ewes in trouble as lambing season was well underway. You can always tell a good farmer by the way that the animals react to him, and in this case they were following his truck as it meandered along; a good sign. He was probably on a 'flipping' run. One thing that pregnant sheep do is occasionally get stuck on their backs. Apparently they roll over to scratch their backs, but when heavily pregnant they get stuck upside down with their feet wriggling skyward. It is called 'flipping' when the farmer grabs them and 'flips' them back onto their feet. Although it looks hilarious it can be dangerous if left for a long time so if you ever see a sheep on its back do flip it as you may save its life, and its baby.

I cruised over the brow of the small hill down towards the Normans Bay railway crossing when two birds caught my eye. I quickly pulled over. These were no normal birds – they were large hunter raptors, super rare, marsh harriers. The pair were stalking crows, which I had never seen before. The crows were feeding in the grass oblivious to what was coming up behind them. The harriers were low to the ground, no more than two feet above it, moving slowly and using the breeze to glide with the odd wing flap. Marsh harriers are an uncommon sight now. They became the landowner's enemy and hunted almost to extinction because of their ability to take larger birds like pheasant and partridge. In recent years they have made a small comeback along our coastal areas as they move in, searching for new breeding grounds. The flatlands and marshes around Pevensey Levels are perfect for them with an abundance of small prey such as field mice, birds and frogs; however the crows rule the roost here and they chase any competition away with a fury.

Crows or corvids are some of the smartest birds and very territorial. Experts tell us that they are the only bird who think a little like humans and because of this many legends and myths surround crows. It was rare to see them being hunted for breakfast. They were at ease pecking and foraging in the wild field grass unaware that coming up behind them was death on the wing. Since raptors had been exterminated in the area the crows has grown large and powerful on the easy pickings and lived at ease all along the flatlands. In fact the carrion crows here are among the largest I have ever seen.

At the last moment one of the harriers, almost behind the crow it was stalking, lifted skyward then pounced onto the back of its unsuspecting prey. All hell broke loose. The young crow was pinned to the ground, screaming and trying to turn, the other harrier rushed over to join in. The cool morning air was broken with the shock of the surprise attack and all the other crows quickly scattered to the skies. However they grouped and circled high in the air. They seemed to communicate with each other and then they came back in force to help their fallen comrade. A family of crows are possibly the only birds I have ever seen do this, their ties are strong. They dropped onto the harriers and assaulted them time after time until the crow that was pinned to the grass managed to wriggle free. Suddenly the hunters became the hunted. The crows attacked the harriers on mass, screaming and squawking as they swept in wave after wave. Even the wounded crow managed to have a go before going to rest on a branch of a crooked tree by the low flint wall in front of me. The harriers could not get air under their wings and scrambled messily away with feathers being ripped and torn from them. I think that they made a lucky escape as I have seen crows kill other birds with their mass attacks. They don't call a group of crows 'a murder of crows' for nothing. With the harriers disappearing into the distance the noisy group returned flapping victoriously back like hooligans after a football match. They landed in the old twisted tree next to the wounded crow that had been attacked. The tree almost turned black in the early light. With a scene that Alfred Hitchcock would have died for in his film The Birds, a mass squawking followed, filling the air with triumphant noise.

Two lessons were learned on the first day of spring over the Pevensey Flatlands. Firstly that the harriers would think twice about attacking a family of crows that would protect each other to the death and secondly the crows found out they had new neighbours that needed very careful watching. If the crows discovered where the harriers were nesting they would kill any chicks and chase them away for good.

Nature is glorious but so cruel. We live in this harsh world surrounded by its beauty and death in equal amounts and as I started the car and rolled down the hill I could not help thinking how lucky I was. I glanced at my watch, all the action had only taken a couple of minutes so I was still on time for my later engagement at Norman's shop.

My first customer was waiting by her bungalow door along the small meandering Ellerslie Lane in Bexhill. She had a bunch of daffodils in her hand that she had just picked. "Alex, spot on time again; I can almost set my watch by you."

"The first call is usually okay," I replied, "It's the rest of the day that falls apart. I hear your Brother Compal Galaxie is talking to you again!"

"She is driving me insane. Keeps telling me that my blue buttonhole lever is extended and I should not continue! I have to stop myself from arguing with it. My husband caught me once and told me he would have me committed if I continue. I mean arguing with a machine, it's like something out of Terminator!"

"You haven't watched Terminator!"

"I've seen them all. I might be 86 but Rise Of The Machines was the business. I've seen it at least three times. Arnie's the best."

"Well who would have believed that Arnold Schwarzenegger had a Bexhill Fan Club. I'll tell him next time I'm having dinner at his house!" We both laughed as we made our way into her bungalow.

Inside I was presented with the annoying machine that had

decided to answer back. Modern technology was mind blowing but every now and then a new fangled gadget comes out that really should not have been invented, and an arguing sewing machine was one of them. Even worse it overruled what you wanted to do, cut the power off so that you could not sew and then with wonderful cut glass words would say, "Do not continue". It was a superb machine but that voice! It drove sewers to distraction.

"ALEX, I have a bone to pick with you," said Ruth, walking menacingly towards me. "Last time you called you told me that Margaret Thatcher did the recording for this machine before she became Prime Minister, when she was working at her father's grocery shop." I was sniggering into my chest but as I looked up she was frowning at me like a school teacher, then suddenly she walloped me.

"Ruth, you didn't really believe me did you?" I said, rubbing my arm.

"Of course I did. I used to tell all my friends about it and we would come to my sewing room and listen to her speak. I would purposely move the buttonhole lever or lift the presser foot and try to sew just so that we could here her tell me off. Yes, I certainly did think that the condescending voice was our dear leader, Margaret. They all told me I was making it up but I assured them that 'my Alex' wouldn't tell porkies, that was until Norman at the sewing shop put me straight. I felt such an idiot and Norman laughed his head off. "Just like Alex," he said, "You know how he likes to pull your leg. Next time you see him give him a good slap."

"So that's from me, and this one's from Norman."

"I almost felt that one," I sniggered after the second feeble blow.

"Now I will need tea before I slip into a coma." Ruth laughed as she went off to put the kettle on. By the time she returned I had found the problem, a small trigger switch on the bobbin winder mechanism that was causing the machine to spurt out incorrect instructions. "I still can't believe that you fell for that old story. I tell everyone that tale but you are the first person who fell for it."

"Well Alex I bet that I am also the first person you have met who has posted her new phone as well!"

"What?"

"Oh yes, I did it all right. Last month I walked down to the post box to post a few letters and while I was walking the phone rang. It was my friend Ruby and as I got to the post box I finished talking, said goodbye with a smile, flipped the cover up and posted it straight into the post box. I looked down at the envelopes in my other hand and wondered why they were still there. Then my jaw dropped. What an idiot, a complete idiot. I stood there for at least a minute thinking that there must be some mistake, I simply could not have done it, but I had, I had posted my new Apple iphone. I sheepishly waited for over two hours for the postman to turn up to collect the midday post so that I could retrieve it. I felt so foolish when he arrived that I think I was as red as the box. Then he told me that it had happened before and went on to tell me some of the weird and wonderful things that he had come across over the years, all stuffed into mail boxes. So yes, I did fall for your stupid 'Thatcher story' hook, line and sinker. Mind you, it is a little funny thinking about it now."

Before long I had finished and I glanced at my watch. I still had two calls before a mad rush to Bexhill town centre to find parking and get to Thimble-Inas. I left Ruth with my best Arnie impression, "I'll be back."

At my next stop I was perched on the end of a large oak farmhouse table fixing a newish Pfaff sewing machine. One by one the family rolled down to breakfast with yawns, greetings and stretches. Before long there was the husband and wife, three daughters, one imminent son-in-law and one partner all tucking into various cereals. "We need loads of bunting and we have two weeks to make it," the mother announced to the table, explaining why a stranger was sitting at the top end fixing her sewing machine. Pre-wedding excitement broke out and the room filled with chatter. I sat back and took a sip of tea. What job on earth could have the tradesman sitting at the breakfast table with the family discussing their wedding; none but mine. It is a privilege to be so readily accepted by strangers and I never tire of it.

Time was slipping by and I had another call to make and still try to get to Normans for eleven. I drove up Endwell Road, which runs parallel to Bexhill railway station just as the school train arrived. By the time I got to the junction with Sea Road a thousand kids filled the streets, most making their way to St Richard's School. Their excited chatter filled the air and their numbers brought all traffic to a temporary standstill, as a sea of grey uniforms poured out of the station across to Magdalen Road and towards St Richard's. Within a moment tomorrow's leaders, workers, mothers and all had disappeared and their enthusiastic banter with them. I chugged up the hill towards Church Street in the Old Town and to 'Nutty Nora'. Nora had a heart of gold but oh my, did she make my life hell. She was as nutty as a Harrods deluxe nut loaf with extra nuts! Today's call would be no different. Nora was in her late 70's and looked like she had just stepped off the set of The African Queen. She was as identical a looking person to Catherine Hepburn as I had ever seen, but the similarity ended there.

I rang the doorbell and braced myself. "Oh Alex, I am so glad you made it. This machine is making me crazy, well more crazy!" We moved inside and I followed her large grey beehive hairdo to the offending Brother embroidery machine. I sat down and stroked her little mongrel that was snuffling by my feet. Toffee was a cross between a Jack Russell and heaven knows what. The dog just looked up at me with long suffering eyes, almost pleading to take her with me as I left. "Before we start I have saved this from your last call, you left it here just after last Christmas." With that Nora handed me a small cheap orange-handled screwdriver, the sort of thing that would fall out of a cracker and would break the first time you used it. "Nora, that's not mine."

"Of course it is, you left it here!"

"Nora, oh never mind, thank you for saving it for me." I gave up trying to convince her as I knew it would be a wasted cause. Nora smiled at her minor triumph and continued, "Now look Alex, as you can see," she said, shaking an instruction book in front of my face. "Pattern number three shows Mickey Mouse with a black head but as much as I try, each time I start the machine Mickey's head comes out red! It is so frustrating, I have read the book backwards with no help. I think it must be a programming error on the circuit board."

"Nora, you have red thread on the sewing machine!"

"Yes."

"Well how can it possibly sew a black head on Mickey if you

have red thread on the machine?"

"Look, I'm not stupid. I am doing pattern number three, the book clearly shows Mickey's head as black."

"But you have red thread on the machine?" I added again as a cold feeling of dread swept over me. It was going to be another long session with Nutty Nora. I looked into her pale eyes and could see no understanding of what I had said. She stared back at me with the look of a kid on her first day in maths class.

"Okay Nora, let's start at the beginning. Where are all your threads?"

It seemed to take forever but in the end I felt that I had given her a basic understanding that the machine would only stitch what thread it had on, regardless of what the book said. Nora looked as if she had been concentrating so hard her brain had burst; her hair was all in tangles and her huge beehive was slipping dangerously to one side. We made two Mickey Mouse figures all in perfect sequence and she re-numbered the book with a large black pen, crossing out the instructions and correcting them so that they were right. I knew I would be back within months and it would be a problem that even a mind-reader would not be able to guess at. As I left Toffee wagged her tail furiously, obviously trying to signal in semaphore a message to be rescued!

It was 10.45am and I had to find parking in the centre of Bexhill. I cruised up and down the streets and managed to squeeze into a spot in Western Road, not too far from Normans. I dragged my toolbox out of the back of car and slammed the large door. A breeze was blowing up from the sea, filling the air with the scent of salty seaweed. I marched up the road with my tool box rubbing against my cords and my work book tucked under my arm. As I walked I took in all the great architecture of the magnificent town. Bexhill was coming to life, the Devonshire Square market was in full swing and the Polish girl running the veg stall was doing a bomb. I love her stuff, the spuds still have mud on them and her veg often has greenfly. Now that is a really good thing as greenfly are so delicate you instantly know that her veg has not been sprayed with some awful chemical or been grown in a hydroponics lab in some heated container.

I stopped to buy a paper from Tracey at the newsagents in St Leonards Road. She makes me smile as most weeks she dresses

Tracey helps run her dad's newsagents. She uses every trick in the book to draw in customers as she tries to compete with the ever creeping presence of the supermarkets. In the summer I have found her in a pirate costume and here at Easter she is serving customers as the Easter Bunny.

in whatever takes her fancy for charity or whatever event is going on at the time. Easter is always 'bunny rabbit' time and she was dressed in a humongous rabbit outfit. Her partner saw me smiling and shouted over to me, "Lost my big game gun, just when I needed it!" Tracey threw him a deadly bunny glance. He sniggered and jokingly hopped away, saying he was off to pick up a sack of carrots for her supper!

Bexhill has a much larger population than people realise and consequently a thriving town centre that seems to have changed little since I was a kid. As the 19th century rolled into the 20th Bexhill expanded at a phenomenal rate with grand houses and plush seafront hotels. These ghosts are still there, if you stop and look up you can see all the faded majestic architecture of the magnificent buildings. Some of the buildings along St Leonards Road and Burford Terrace would look quite happy as great manor houses if they were transplanted into a rural setting. I was staring

Many of the superb buildings in St Leonards Road, Bexhill, were completed in 1912, the year the Titanic went down. Although in poor repair they have a faded elegance and would look at home in several European capitals.

at a lead drainpipe with a 1912 date on it when I remembered I needed to get a wriggle on.

I power walked into Norman's just as a customer was plonking a machine onto his counter. "Perfect timing Alex," said Norman as I put my tools down and caught my breath. Like a Swiss watch the morning had worked perfectly, now all I had to do was repair Norman's machines and then down to Di Paolo's for a break and the best latte in Bexhill.

An hour later I walked into Di Paolo's opposite the stunning art

Norman Jacobs runs one of the most vibrant haberdashery shops that I have the pleasure of visiting. Thimble-Inas is an explosion of colour and excitement. The shop is bang up to date with the latest computer sewing machines but also stuffed with traditional fabrics and products.

deco De La Warr Pavilion on Bexhill seafront. I was going to write that it looks like it had just fallen out of a Hercule Poirot movie but then I remembered that it has actually been featured in at least one of them. Walking out of Di Paolo's was Luigi and his father John, so I braced myself for the usual offensive. "Ciao Alex, dobbiamo rimanere uniti." I use to have no idea what he was talking about and I always bluffed my way by him with enthusiastic hand waving and smiles, but this time I stopped to chat before going into the welcoming café. Di Paolo's had been run by the same Italian family for generations and John spoke perfect English but now and again he would throw a bit of Italian out to please his customers. The café was a little bit of Italy on a quiet corner of Bexhill and, as with all great Italian Cafés, their award winning ice creams were to die for.

As I entered the café Joe was serving behind the counter, a tall

Di Paolo's Café, opposite the grand De La Warr Pavilion, is one of the finest café's on the coast. Family run for generations it is a great place for a coffee or one of Luigi's award winning handmade ice creams. Here are some of the family, Joe on the left seems to be able to remember all of his customer's names and their drinks, while Luigi, standing second from the right next to his dad John and brother Pas, makes ice cream to die for.

well-built man with a great sense of humour and a personal touch with his regulars. He has some amazing part of his brain that can remember not only his customer's names but their favourite snacks and drinks. It was after I had been accosted a few times by his uncle that I asked Joe what he was talking about. He explained that we both shared a full head of hair! He was so proud of his hair (typical Italian) that he mentioned it every time we met and basically he was saying that there was not many of us left so we had to stick together. What a compliment, my mum always told me I had horse hair! Luckily as I had aged it stayed with me. When I first found out what John was saying I burst out laughing. Not in a million years had it been close to what I imagined.

Just as Joe was pouring my drink and telling me the average age in Bexhill was about 110, little Sid hobbled in. "See what I mean," Joe whispered with a smile. "Morning Sid" shouted Joe down the counter. Sid nodded and then looked up at me. "Well if it ain't old fannyfernakerpan, how you doing boy?" Sid did not wait for a reply. "Come and sit down with me, I have a great story to tell you. Coffee and two toast Joe, and easy on the milk. Oh me bleedin' 'nees, give me strength." Sid hobbled off to a seat and I soon followed with my frothy latte.

It was Sid who gave me the great story about Albert Blake and how he saved Eastbourne during World War Two, as well as his skinny dipping with girls from the Armed Forces. His tale in my book Have I Got A Story For You was one of the most popular ones and his way of telling it was pure magic.

Sid was a Londoner through and through and spoke with the

cockney tongue learnt on the back streets of the great city. Often when I called to fix his wife Eve's sewing machine he would tell tales of such colour that I would be transported back in time to the streets of 1940's London. Today would be no different.

I sat down with Sid and took a great big breath. I had been rushing on the tightest of schedules since before it was light and for the first time I could relax. I sugared my drink and prepared myself, for if there was ever a great story teller it was Little Sid.

LITTLE SID

Over the years I had absorbed a lot of information about Little Sid and his early life in London. Like old nursery rhymes, many details had stuck in my mind. Now, as we sat in Di Paolo's, he was going to add to them with an amazing incident during World War Two, which earned him a medal.

Sid Day was born in Lamlash Street, just off the Elephant & Castle in London. Little Sid never let on exactly in which year he was born, but from our many conversations I had guesstimated that it must have been in the late 1920's. His memories of London in the early days of his youth all point to around 1928. There is a reason that he was reluctant about the date of his birth as I shall explain later. Anyway, Sid was born just along the road from, and a few years before, that great Cockney actor Maurice Joseph Micklewhite, or as we know him today, Michael Caine. Like Sid he had grown up around Southwark. Sid always talked as if they were mates from the Smoke who walked the same streets and sang the same Cockney songs.

110

The Elephant & Castle is one of the older parts of London and Sid told me that it got its name from a gift to King Henry III way back around 1255. Apparently King Louis IX of France gave Henry an elephant, not seen in England since Roman times. Henry was a collector of rare animals, which he kept in his private zoo in The Tower of London. Sid laughed when he told me to ignore the history books because all the local lads knew that the Elephant was not kept at The Tower, but in a specially built viewing arena south of the river. People would travel down to Southwark, to see the Elephant 'from the Castle' and the area eventually became known as The Elephant & Castle. Today it is simply called The Elephant. I always loved it when Sid told me his version of history and I had to wonder which was more accurate; local oral history which was passed down by word of mouth over the centuries, or some dry researcher's book which once written, was parroted ever after. Anyway, whatever the truth of the area, Little Sid grew up there; a true Cockney Londoner and I'll give some clarifications to his Cockney as we go.

Sid's dad was also called Sid. So as Sid grew he became known by all and sundry as Little Sid (and his dad Big Sid), though in truth neither of them grew much above five feet tall! Times were as hard as they could be in the 1930's and many went hungry. The winters were bitter with no heating and jobs were few and far between. When Mosley and his Blackshirts walked the streets many took the pound pay he was offering to wear his armband, even though they didn't give a hoot for his politics.

"Now boy," said Sid as he wriggled on his chair in the café, "I'm going to tell you a story of 'ow I got me first medal. As the war started there had been a huge evacuation of kids from around my

111

area and most of the schools closed," he said as he started yet another tale of his colourful life. "I was just too young to work and too old to be evacuated. London became a ghost town for yun'un's and I wandered the streets looking for something to do. Life were miserable when you had no greens (greens-green-gages-wages). We may 'ave 'ad a poor education but we were streetwise and usually found some mischief to get up to. Anyways, after a few months some of my friends came back as nothing was happening with the war. The blackout was in full force and after dark it was as black as Nudies Knocker. Most of the motorised transport had been taken for the war effort so London went back to the horse and cart. For a while I used to go around with our local vet as he despatched the old and knackered horses. We travelled in an open cart with his bolt gun, around Southwark sorting out the injured and lame. Some survived and were treated and some went to the local butchers shops and glue makers. We ate well for a while! You ever had horse meat, boy?"
"Can't say I have Sid. Is it any good?"
"If you cook it right it's edible but I wouldn't swap it for a pot of jellied eels or pie and mash. Anyways, then rationing hit and hard times got even harder. Two ounces of cheese a week, two ounces of butter and fat, and one bleedin' egg. Mum could have a pound of sugar a month to make jam 'n stuff like that. Luckily we all kept rabbits and caught eels from the rivers and canals. There were another little bonus to those that knew – pigeons. Tasty little treat a pigeon and if there was one place that there were plenty it was the parks and squares around London. Mind you, there were a knack. Getting them to take the grain while you were near enough to grab 'em, then a quick twist of the neck and in the bag for dinner. Three could feed us like kings.

Anyways, I was about thirteen or so when fate took a hand. All hell broke out and what you lot call The Blitz started. Bombs fell like rain and it were only a matter of time before we copped one. When it 'appened we all survived but the house was flattened. Scurvy, my yellow canary was blown out of its cage. I found 'im shakin' in the gutter down the street wiv' most his feavers missin'! While my dad helped dig out our neighbours we grabbed any bits of furniture worth saving and bundled what we could onto a cart and headed for shelter. We got re-housed down the road just off the A3 in De Laune Street Flats in Kennington. Hardly out of 'arms way, but it was all they had.

Now 'ere's where the fun starts boy. When we were bombed I lost my birth certificate. That was bad news as no certificate meant no rations, which meant the soup kitchen on the corner of Cooks Road for me most nights. Then fate played a hand. When my temporary Birth Certificate arrived they messed up the dates making me over two years older. Well, I rushed off to the Post Office and registered it sharpish like. Suddenly I was sixteen and the world was me oyster. Now I could get a job and earn some dosh so I wouldn't be boracic (boracic lint, skint). Being short I managed to get a job stoking a boiler on a steam lorry; didn't take up much room, see.

It took nearly an hour to get the boiler up to steam so while it was buildin' we would load up our goods and then, each morning before sun-up, we would drive into London to make our deliveries. It were a dirty job, but fun. One big problem wiv' the lorry was it 'ad solid tyres and slid like a brick on ice when it was wet. The brakes 'ardly slowed us so Bert would jam the lorry into the kerb to slow it down. I would hold on for dear life while he swore like the old sailor he was. At the end of the week I got me first goose's (goose neck, cheque) and blew it all wiv' me mates.

Bert was always telling me about life at sea and it sounded good. Then I had a brainwave and applied for the Navy. They were desperate and looking for short lads for the subs. I thought there would be no 'arm in trying, so loaded with my new birth certificate I 'ad a go. Mum and Dad said if they were stupid enough to let me in, they wouldn't stop me, so I managed to bluff my way in and started me trainin'. The first weekend on leave I came home in uniform and almost floated up the street. My Mum came out to greet me and I felt like the Pearly King of the East End. It didn't last. Somehow the Navy got wise and sent me packing, but it was fun while I was there. I knew that as soon as I could I'd join up again.

So there I was back in London wiv' all the bombing still going on, and no job. By now all the services were pulling together to try and keep the city going, so I got a job taking messages around London. Communications were all over the place with the damage, so the most reliable way turned out to be the simplest. Messages, from each section of the city, were written on paper then sent by bicycle to The Ministry letting them know what damage had been done. Then they coordinate rescue and repairs. I would collect all the messages from the different sections in my area and then take them to Whitehall on my bike.

I used to cycle around the bomb-blitzed city, pedalling like a maniac so The Huns didn't get me with their bleedin' stick bombs. Most of the damage reports were collected at night and

114

you gotta remember boy, there was a complete blackout. You could see more when the bombing was 'appenin as the lads with the anti-aircraft guns were throwing muck up at the planes and the planes were dropping bombs on us, lighting up the streets right proper. It was one hell of a time but I tell you now boy, I'd give everything I own to be back there right now.

Life fell into a bit of a routine as the war rumbled on. During the day search and rescue dug out the bodies, teams cleared the rubble and patched the roads, and we all carried on in a shared spirit of survival. That was until one night, the night I won me medal."

Sid had been talking almost non-stop as he ate and drank opposite me in Di Paulo's and I was loving every minute of it, he had me grasped in his little fat hands and I was itching for him to continue. As Sid talked he would gesture this way and that, his arms flying up in the air with a coffee in one hand and toast in the other. I looked over at Joe behind the counter and he was leaning on his arms with a teatowel over his shoulder, listening to every word. Sid's eyes sparkled with his lost youth as he continued.

"I fink it must 'ave been about June 'cause the nights were short. Anyways one night I was cycling along with my messages, I had one more pick up at Station Fourteen when I looked up to see something strange hurtling through the spotlights in the sky. At first I thought it was a plane going down, but this was different. It turned out to be a Buzz Bomb or a Doodlebug. The first I 'ad seen of the V1 rockets. People were running for the underground shelter at Kennington Park Underground when it came down. Like an idiot I just stared at it until it hit. Mother of Mercy did it make the ground shake. The whole area lit up in the most horrendous colours as if the door of Hell had opened, and then a complete blackness. When everything had calmed down an eerie silence came over the area. We had all seen something terrible for the very first time. I tell you boy, we had already seen some damn awful stuff but them V1's were the worst. In the blackness I forgot about picking up the messages and went to see what had happened.

I cycled along, wobbling around all the rubble as best as I could in the dark, until I came round the Johnnie (Johnnie Horner, corner) and there were the biggest hole I'd ever seen, just next to Orn's Public House, opposite Kennington Park. The hole must have been twenty feet deep, maybe more. I stood on the edge and as much as I waved my bike light I couldn't see the bottom.

116

To make matters worse I suddenly realised I got a bit of shrapnel in my leg, which didn't help. It was probably the muck from our ack-ack guns as most of the bombers had gone. I'm pretty sure I was hit by friendly fire! It wasn't too bad but it made me hobble. I was sitting on some rubble in the smoke in the pitch black, shining my bike light down on me leg, wundrin' what Mum was going to say when she saw the blood on me trousers, when I heard a bleedin' bus coming!

Well, now I'm in a state of panic. The bus was heading straight for the hole in the ground and if they went in, they weren't coming out alive. I hobbled into the road waving my blackout light as much as I could but they didn't see me. I quickly unscrewed the lens cover and waved it again, shouting at the top of me voice. I heard the brakes of the bus go on and jumped out of the way as it squealed past. I thought the lot were dun fer. It ground to a halt not six feet away from the hole. Behind it were three more cars that had been following the bus in the dark.

A huge black limo slid up to me and the driver wound down his window and asked my name. I just said 'Sid sir. Post Fourteen sir'. He wound up the window and drove away. Anyway the bus went on its way and I picked up the last of the messages and cycled into the city to deliver them. I was an hour late wiv me bad leg 'n all but I made it and went home to be patched up by my Mum.

Next day I was directing traffic outside Station Fourteen feelin' a bit sorry for myself when I got a message from the Duty Sergeant that I was to report to him right sharpish. I hobbled over to his office and he was as red as a bleedin' beetroot, fresh from the boiler. "WHAT THE 'ELL 'AVE YOU BEEN UP TO SID? I've 'ad the bloody Ministry Of Defence on the line all morning asking me questions about you?"

"Nuffin' Sir. Promise Sir."

"So you weren't stopping buses last night down the road then eh? Wavin' a bleeding non-regulation bike light at them!"

"Oh Sir. I 'ad to stop it or they would 'ave perished for sure!"

"Perished for sure, eh Sid."

"Yes Sir, sure as 'Enry cut Anne's 'ed orf."

"Did someone in a limo talk to you?"

"A driver did Sir, but I saw nuffin of nobody in the back sir. Black as Nudies Knocker it was Sir."

"Well Sid, seems that you've made a friend for yourself up at the Palace. Bloody War Office want to give you a medal! Get a suit and get your arse up to Windsor tonight. Report to the door with this note."

"With that, me boss shook my hand, patted me on the back, and kicked me out of his office. That night I went up to Windsor Castle for Flags Night and got me my first medal for bravery. I was wearing me Dad's suit that me Mum 'ad pinned up, and I was so nervous I could hardly remember what 'appened. All them 'big wigs' all dressed up to the nines wiv' so much spit and polish it made my eyes bulge. I 'ad such a night I can't even remember how I got home.

Anyways, filled wiv' enthusiasm I went back and enrolled again in The Royal Navy, this time telling them my real age. What wiv' all me experience wiv' subs and wiv' me London job and me medal, they let me in. Well, I soon shot up the ranks and 'ad three stripes in no time at all. After I came out of The Royal Navy I went up to Buck 'ouse and taught life-saving techniques as part of The Royal Life Saving Society. But that's another story for another day." said Sid, banging his cup down on the table as if he had been drinking gin in some shady bar in the back of beyond.

I felt myself letting out a deep sigh, as if I had just been to see the best film of the year and it was now over. I looked up at Joe and he was just smiling. He leaned over and said "Tell Alex about the Foreign Legion, Sid,"
"Aw I'm knackered now, I need me forty winks and me bleedin' knees are killin' me."
Sid took the last sip of his drink, folded up a half slice of toast and rolled it into his gob. "Any chance of a lift home, boy?" He asked, spitting out crumbs as he talked.
"Of course, Sid. I'm going your way anyway."

I helped Sid up into my Land Rover, "Sweet Jesus 'ow the 'ell do you get up into this thing without a ladder?"
"It's all technique, Sid" I laughed as we rumbled by The De La Warr Pavilion. Before long I was pulling up to Sid's place. Eve, his wife, was weeding in the garden and came over to help Sid out of the car.
"Has he been bothering you again, Alex?"
"I've loved every second, Eve. I could listen to Sid all day. Next time he's going to tell me about The Foreign Legion."
"Oh that's a good one, Alex. I never get tired of that. I'm amazed they didn't put him up against a wall and shoot him."

Sid wrapped his arm around Eve in that way that only lovers can and together they toddled off down the path, Sid wobbling along like a penguin, his bent old knees almost audibly creaking as he went. When he got to the door he turned and waved to me, "Don't forget we gotta take me boat up the river when we get the chance."

"That's a date, Sid. Let me know when there's a fair wind blowing."

Post Script

I never did get the chance to sail up the River Rother where Sid had his boat, and he never did get the chance to tell me about his further adventures with the Foreign Legion. Eve rang later in the year to say that Sid had finally given up and gone to his big ship in the sky. Little Sid, my five foot London Cockney with the heart of gold, had gone forever and we all miss him dearly.

SAD OLD SOLDIER

S. O. S.

I sit in old obscurity with my aching bones,
Hidden from the living where no one ever phones.
I peek through curtain slits while neighbours come and go,
And wonder what I've done to life for it to treat me so.
As one more day slips away with the telly full of moans,
I sit in old obscurity and rub my aching bones.

A I A

ROLLIN' IN THE DIRT

Some days I feel like I could live forever.
Some days I feel like I have!
A I A

May had arrived with high winds and slashing rain. My calls had swung by with ease and Tuesday had started much the same. I had a packed day and if all went well I would cover over 100 miles and fix many machines all around my little corner of East Sussex.

My first visit was to a brown-eyed beauty whose industrial Juki sewing machine was in bits. "I watched a YouTube video on how to repair my machine," she announced with a bright smile.
"Didn't work then!" I laughed staring at all the parts scattered on the table.
"It turned out to be a bit trickier than I thought, but I have been told if anyone can get it working you can" she threw back at me, with a beam across her face and a set of teeth straight out of a Colgate advert.
"I bet you get away with murder don't you?"

"Not always Alex, not always." She laughed, swung her head back and sashayed off towards the kitchen where the kettle was whistling up a treat. I shook my head and got stuck into the tricky job of rebuilding the hook mechanism on her machine. Over the last few years YouTube had been the bane of my life, as so called experts from around the world showed people how to fix their sewing machines. What they never expressed or understood was that a sewing machine is a fantastic piece of highly complex engineering and to get a machine perfectly balanced you are working with tolerances no thicker than a piece of hair. The result is that many of my calls that would have been relatively easy, had turned into major rebuilds.

This is the only sign that the great man lived at Windlesham Manor, a small plaque near the front door to the rest home.

An hour or so later I passed Windlesham Manor on the back road to Crowborough. I smiled to myself when I thought back to Arthur Conan Doyle and the lovely house that he designed and built. After his death in July of 1930 he was buried in his favourite spot, his rose garden overlooking his beloved golf course. However what few people know was that he was buried standing up! It was a strange request and did not last long for in 1955 he was moved down to Minstead in the New Forest and I guess this time they really did 'lay' him to rest. He wasn't happy about it as his ghost still haunts the area. One of my customers told me all about meeting it and I wrote her spine chilling story down in my book Have I Got A Story For You. It's called (not surprisingly) The Ghost of Arthur Conan Doyle.

As I slowly threaded my way down a bumpy farm track towards my next customer I spotted a large black crow edging its way towards a new born rabbit that was busy nibbling grass. I hooted my horn and the rabbit disappeared at the speed of light into some stinging nettles. The crow threw a black-eyed stare at me and flapped off in disgust. His family had probably lived around here for a thousand years, for Crowborough gets its name from these cunning birds and was once known as 'the place of the crows'. I guess I had interrupted his breakfast; good thing too. Mother Nature may be 'red in tooth and claw' but I was happy to save the life of one baby rabbit on my way to work.

A mile further down the endless track I stopped again. I spotted a herd of deer grazing in a field. I quietly slipped out, clicked the car door closed and crept along the hedgerow with my camera. The wet rain and warm sun had made the earth smell glorious and my world in East Sussex was growing by the second. Every

East Sussex is still heavily forested in places. On my early calls I often spot wild deer grazing the corners of fields. They always stick close to the tree line and scarper at the first sign of trouble.

leaf and blade of grass was on a mission to expand into the new summer, capturing as much light as possible before autumn came once more. Before the deer caught a sniff of me I snapped a couple of shots. They scarpered towards the forest and within seconds blended invisibly into the tree line.

It still never ceases to amaze me how inspiring this place is, this 'Goldilocks Planet' as the scientists call her, that is so perfectly placed in our solar system, watered, blown and basted by just enough sun and rain as we turn on some invisible barbecue spit in space. Today was another wonderful day on planet Earth and I was lapping it up.

Above the dense forest canopy two buzzards circled. I knew from where they were that they could survey countless miles of open land all the way down to the coast, for Crowborough is one of the highest places in my area. I jumped back in the Disco and carried along the bumpy track. Before long I spotted the entrance to the stables where I knew three industrial machines were waiting, and as I was to find out a few other surprises as well!

A pack of Alsatians started barking like mad, causing havoc in the yard. I saw the owners rushing around, trying to get them all locked away, leaving just one small shabby-haired terrier cross. The dog stood enquiringly at the gate with her big dark eyes staring at me and her tail wagging like a windscreen wiper on overdrive. Teresa came back out of a barn whistling like a lumberjack, swung open the five-bar and ushered me into the yard. "She won't bite, no teeth left," she laughed. Her husband closed the gate behind me and whispered through the open window, "A whistlin' woman and a crowin' hen brings the devil from his den." I smiled but said nothing. After getting out of my car I let the dog sniff me and tickled the mutt behind its ear. Its round black eyes became like small almonds as it leaned its head into my hand with great satisfaction. "I can see that you're alright with animals then," nodded Teresa approvingly.
"Oh yes, I think I would have been out of business 30 years ago if I didn't get along with most animals." Visions of the odd killer mutt biting me rushed through my mind but in the countless calls over the years I had only been bitten three times, so I had a pretty

good track record. Mind you I was happy that Teresa had locked up the pack of Alsatians. They were barking their heads off trying to see what was going on and however much the owners shouted at them it simply added to the noise rather than reduced it.

Have you ever seen such a crazy goat? It seemed harmless but had a menacing leer as it moved closer to me. I quickly got inside the barn but that ended up worse!

I spotted a huge male goat staring at me through the barbed wire. Funnily my first thought was how much it looked like Princess Leia out of Star Wars with its big bun ears. He had twisted spiralling horns around a foot long and jammed onto each horn was a tennis ball. I had to smile knowing that the little devil probably caused havoc around the farm. I took in a deep breath for all farms have their own scent, a mixture of animals and feed that has probably been much the same since humans decided to domesticate wild beasts.

I was taken to one of the stables in the barn where the three machines were all covered by blankets. Teresa explained the problem with each machine, adding at the end of each sentence that they had once worked! So did my back, I thought, remembering how easy it used to be to touch my toes or tie my laces. Now touching my toes was a distant memory and even tying my shoelaces had become an art that required copious amounts of tongue hanging out.

I sat at the first machine and threw off the blanket. Big mistake! I was mercilessly showered with dust, horse hair and all the other debris that collects in barns. The large dark horse in the stable opposite me whinnied as if to laugh at my misfortune. I coughed and looked down at my new M&S cords which had instantly gone from smart navy blue to farmyard brown. Too late to worry now I thought to myself, and it was probably going to be worse by the time I finished.

I opened my toolbox displaying the layers of carefully placed tools, specialist tools of the trade, some even made to order for me. I sighed, rested my glasses on the end of my nose and got down to work. About half an hour later I heard the uncomfortable sound of Teresa unbolting the door to the dogs. Admittedly they had all calmed down and she assured me that they were totally safe. The pack came excitedly into my stable, pushing each other forward trying to get to me. Now, single dogs are usually a breeze but put them in a pack and you never know what is going to happen. One of the mutts trod on the edge of my toolbox, catapulting some of my tools out onto the stable floor. Crap, I thought, and lurched forward into the pack to try and pull the rest of my precious toolbox away before more damage occurred.

The lull before the storm. Like many farms Teresa's is no different, stuff everywhere and filled with the smells that all working farms have. Her machines have not only to survive in that hostile environment but work perfectly on her horse rugs and tarpaulins. Here I am shortly before she let the dogs out and I got plastered in all sorts of foul things.

Next thing I knew one of the mutts had nudged me from behind in a delicate area and I was pushed to my knees in the dirt. I bent over trying to protect my half closed toolbox.

Oh it gets worse! In all the madness that was going on, all the barking and the shoving, the sniffing, licking and the nudging, one of the mutts decided to stick its foul tongue down my throat! I was filthy, gagging, spitting, coughing and dribbling on my knees. In walked Teresa who laughed, "We won't get that muck off with a damp cloth will we? Time for a cuppa tea yet Alex?" Then she disappeared chuckling to herself, without the slightest effort to call the dogs away. Maybe she thought it would save her having to walk them?

Two hours later I had finally finished my work. I stank; I was covered from head to foot in dog, goat and horse hair, oil and dirt. I itched all over but, like a true pro, I had three sewing machines all humming like new. Ah, the sweet smell of success against all the odds. The dogs, that had caused all the chaos, were lounging around like lords after an orgy and even the horses had lost interest in what I was doing. I did a couple of rug repairs for Teresa to show her how to get the best out of each different machine and walked out of the barn into the sunshine. In the yard I brushed off what muck I could and clambered back into my Disco. I sparked her up and headed for home. I had long given up on the idea of continuing with my calls, I needed to go straight home to have a shower and bung my clothes in the wash or maybe just burn them! I would make my apologies to my other customers and catch up with them later in the week.

As I drove the smell of a working stables clung to me, even with all the windows open. Within the hour I was home and ran up to the shower, throwing off my clothes as I went. There was still just enough lukewarm water left from the mornings heating to wash most of the smell and dirt away. Clean, I ate a sandwich and in my mind's eye went over the ridiculous events of the morning.

As I had driven away from Teresa's, she slammed the gate she shouted, "This'll be a good one for your next book!" How right she was I thought. I might not have time to fix anymore sewing machines but I had time for a story.

I rushed to the keyboard and started hammering away at my latest tale that just had to be called Rollin' in the Dirt.

A Brief History of the Sewing Machine
By Alex Askaroff

"One of the few useful things ever invented"
Mahatma Gandhi

Who invented the sewing machine? It is a question I am often asked in my profession and I have spent endless hours researching it. Let me take you on a brief and fascinating tour of one of the most worthwhile inventions of the 19th century.

By the middle of the Victorian era sewing machines were taking hold in America, and within the space of a few years they had spread across the globe. Before that period all fabric would have been joined by hand; every single stitch using methods hardly changed since Stone Age times. Clothes were slow and timely to produce and cost a lot of money. Factories around the world were employing people (mainly women because they were better at it) to sew all day long. As the population of our planet exploded and the Industrial Revolution took hold, someone had to come up with a solution of how to join two pieces of fabric quicker and cheaper than by hand. This in turn led to a captivating trail of invention and failure. Some inventors died in poverty, some became rich beyond their dreams. One man, Singer, became so famous that his name is still one of the most well-known names all over the world.

So how did it all begin? First of all I want you to read a quote from one of the first sewing machine pioneers, James Edward Allen Gibbs. James was the son of a Shenandoah farmer and witnessed all the major developments of the sewing machine. In 1901 he was an old man and was interviewed about his inventions and patents. No other person alive was better qualified to quote on the subject and his words are absolutely crucial in understanding the development of the sewing machine.

"No useful sewing machine was ever invented by one man; and all first attempts to do work by machinery, previously done by hand, had been failures. It was only after several able inventors had failed in their attempts, that someone with the mental powers to combine the efforts of others, with his own, at last produced a practicable sewing machine."

Sewing machine manufacturing started slowly and was constantly interrupted. However in the 50 years from 1846 to 1896 the sewing machine went from a circus attraction to a necessity for every household. The Victorian era, with its massive expansion in industry and technology proved to be the fertile ground in which the sewing machine grew.

The first mention of mechanical sewing was in England in 1755.

Charles Weisenthal was German but while living in England he took out a patent for a needle to be used for 'mechanical sewing'. Unfortunately we do not know what sort of mechanical sewing it was as description of the machine was not properly mentioned in his patent.

In 1790, once more in England, Thomas Saint really cracked it. Not only did he patent a sewing machine but also he provided enough of a description so that a replica could be built and, once modified, stitch. British Patent No. 1764 was awarded to the London cabinetmaker. Due to other patents he filed dealing with leather, the patent was with "Glues & Varnishes" and not discovered until 1873, when the British sewing machine pioneer, Newton Wilson came across it while researching the history of the sewing machine.

In 1804 we go to France, where Thomas Stone had patented a machine that we know little about. That must have been a good year as we have two other gentlemen on the scene; a James Henderson and a canny Scotsman, Mr Duncan, who had plans for an embroidery machine. Again, nothing has ever come to light about their machines.

Around 1810, Balthasar Krems came up with a unique sewing machine, which he used to sew the seams of caps he was manufacturing. His sewing machine was pedal operated and sewed a continuous circular chain stitch. There is one of his machines at the Eifel museum in Mayen, Germany, and another replica at the Deutsche Museum in Munich. Because old Balthasar did not patent his design we cannot be sure of the exact dates, but we do know he was German, ya vol! The Germans hold him as the inventor of the sewing machine.

Now we travel across the border to the land of schnitzel and lederhosen, Austria. The year is 1814, Napoleon is about to meet his Waterloo and Josef Madersperger, a humble tailor is building

In 1950, the Austrians, who still claim to have invented the sewing machine, produced a run of stamps featuring their inventor Josef Madersperger.

the first of several machines. Although he had been working on his machine since 1807 it was not until 1815 that he was granted patent rights. He tried in vain for years to get his machine right and in 1839 he almost cracked it. In 1841 his machine was awarded a bronze medal but he could not find a manufacturer to produce it. Josef had invested every penny in his invention and spent his life working on it. He was however still making the same old mistake that many early pioneers made, which was trying to make his machine copy the hand movement of sewing girls.

Eventually Josef gave his model away and a few years later, in 1850, he died a pauper in the poorhouse in Vienna. The Austrians hold him as the inventor of the sewing machine.

Hold on I hear you shouting! What about America! Well at last we come to the land of the free and the home of the brave.

In 1818 John Knowles and his partner, John Adams Doge, made a sewing machine and it really stitched! But there is a catch. The machine would only stitch a few inches of cloth before it had to be reset, which turned out to be as time-consuming as sewing by hand.

In 1826, Henry Lye of Philadelphia, Pennsylvania, patented a sewing machine of sorts but fire destroyed the patent office and his invention was lost, so we move on again.

In 1829-30 the first real sewing machine that we know about was born in France. Barthelemy Thimonnier (I'm going to call him Bart as it makes my head hurt spelling his name) took out a

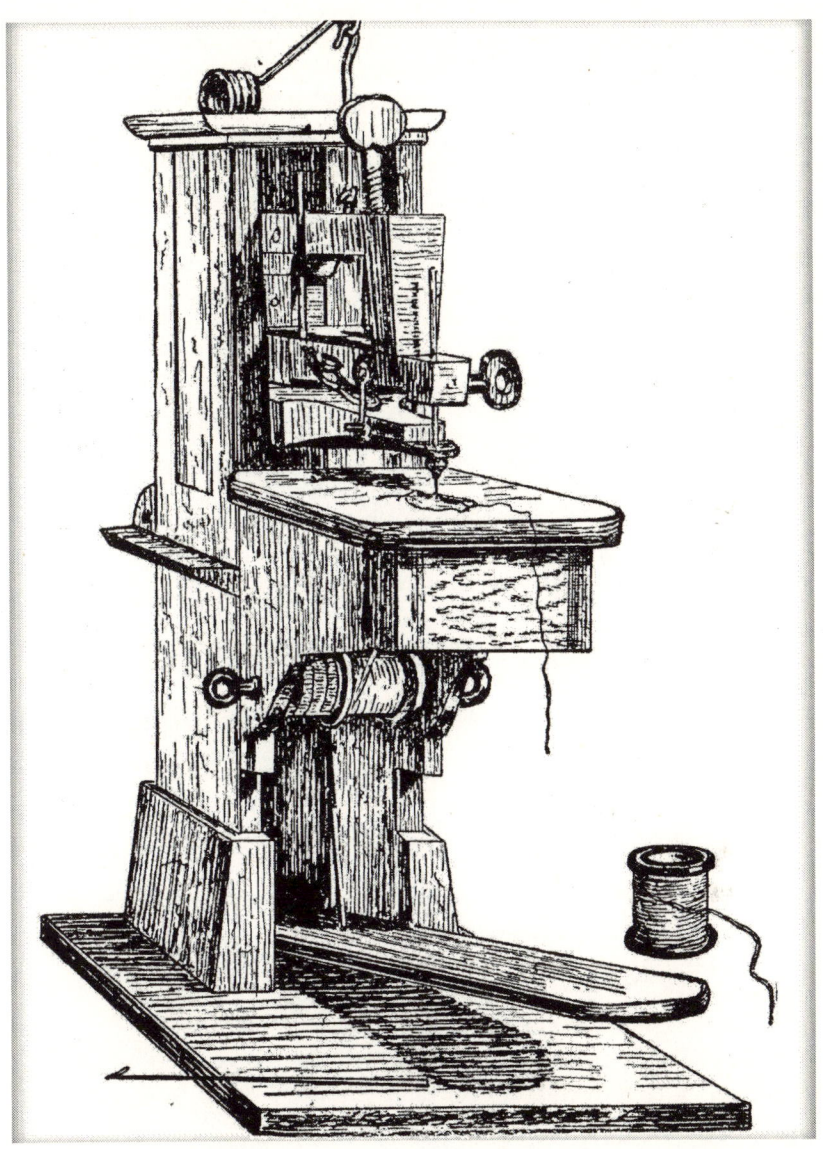

Barthelemy Thimonnier's machine was a sort of sewing machine but in reality it was a strange contraption that was doomed to failure.

patent for a barbed needle, a bit like a fish hook, to be used in his sewing machine.

Bart's machine was not a hit with the French tailors. The machine, made mainly of wood, actually worked. In fact it worked so well that he used them to sew uniforms for the French army.

Before long Bart was sewing away with dozens of machines, taking work from the hungry tailors of Paris. We all know what Frenchmen are like when their blood is up, Madame Guillotine was still warm from their revolution. In 1831 it all came to a head in his workshop at Rue de Sevres, where 80 of his wooden machines were busily sewing away. The angry tailors gathered outside Bart's premises, stormed in and burnt the lot.

Bart fled to England but never regained his former success. For several years he tried in vain to sell his ideas and in 1845 teamed up with the son of a solicitor to try again but by 1850, with his improved American patent granted he just never got the break he needed. Broke again he eventually sold some of his patents to a company in Manchester. Although he had made the first reasonable sewing machine it did not stop the old tailor ending up like his Austrian counterpart.

Poor old Bart died in poverty in Amplepuis on the 5th of August 1857. The French still hold him as the inventor of the sewing machine.

Back in America things were on the boil. In 1834 Walter Hunt was in his basement in New York arguing with his daughter,

Frances, about taking work from the poor sewing women. Walter had made a sewing machine that produced a lockstitch and his daughter was not happy about it. It was a brand new design and worked! It even had two spools of thread. However he never patented it and then sold the plans. Walter was one of the most prolific inventors of his time but nearly always sold his ideas before patenting them and therefore is hardly remembered today.

Actually Walter Hunt will always go down in history, not for the sewing machine but for another 'point', he invented the safety pin! Sorry I couldn't resist that little joke.

In 1841 Newton and Archibald, back in England, had designed a chain-stitch machine employing an eye-pointed needle, but little else is known of the invention.

On 21 February 1842, John James Greenough of Washington DC patented a sewing machine with a stitch forming mechanism. Patent 2466 was the first ever American patent for a sewing machine. It had a device for presenting work onto a double pointed needle with an eye in the middle. I bet he pricked his fingers a few times!

In 1843, Dr Frank Goulding of Macon, Georgia also created a sewing device but once again he failed to develop it.

In 1844, back in England again, John Fisher patented a lace making machine that sewed. However, the patent was misfiled and John did not pursue his invention.

Our trail of failure is all going to change when in 1844 a young

Massachusetts farmer was about to shake the sewing world. Elias Howe finished his sewing engine in 1844 and had enough money to patent it by 1846. Elias's machine was a cracker and most modern day sewing machines use some of his principles. 1846 is probably the most important date in the history of sewing and

Patented in 1846 this machine embodied the principles of the sewing machine and some are still in use to this day. Elias patented several important features that made it very difficult for any manufacturer to make a sewing machine without infringing on his patents. If there was one man in history that could be said to have invented the sewing machine in principle, it was Elias Howe.

the true birth of the sewing machine. The Americans hold him as the inventor of the sewing machine.

Elias tried in vain to sell his expensive and weird contraption but it had no takers in America, so he travelled to England where his brother, Amasa, had found a possible purchaser. All this ended in tears and disappointment and Elias headed home broke. On arriving back in America he found things had changed. In his absence sewing machines had hit the big time. Dozens of sewing machine companies had sprung up and many of them were using his patents, including one Mr Singer.

Most of us know the name Singer but few are aware of his amazing story, his rags to riches journey from a little runaway to one of the richest men of his age. The story of Isaac Merritt Singer will blow your mind; his wives and lovers, castles and countless children, all built on the back of one of the greatest inventions of the 19th century.

Now Elias, unlike nearly all the other inventors who gave up, was stubborn and determined. He borrowed money and sued everyone he could, including our most famous sewing machine entrepreneur, Isaac Singer. In 1850 Isaac had won a bet (so he said) to make a better sewing machine than was available on the market. It was patented in 1851 and changed the world as we know it because it was better than anything else. It was probably Singer that James Gibbs was referring to at the start of our story. The first reliable sewing machine, with a guarantee, had arrived on planet earth.

Elias Howe was poor at selling but brilliant in court and made a

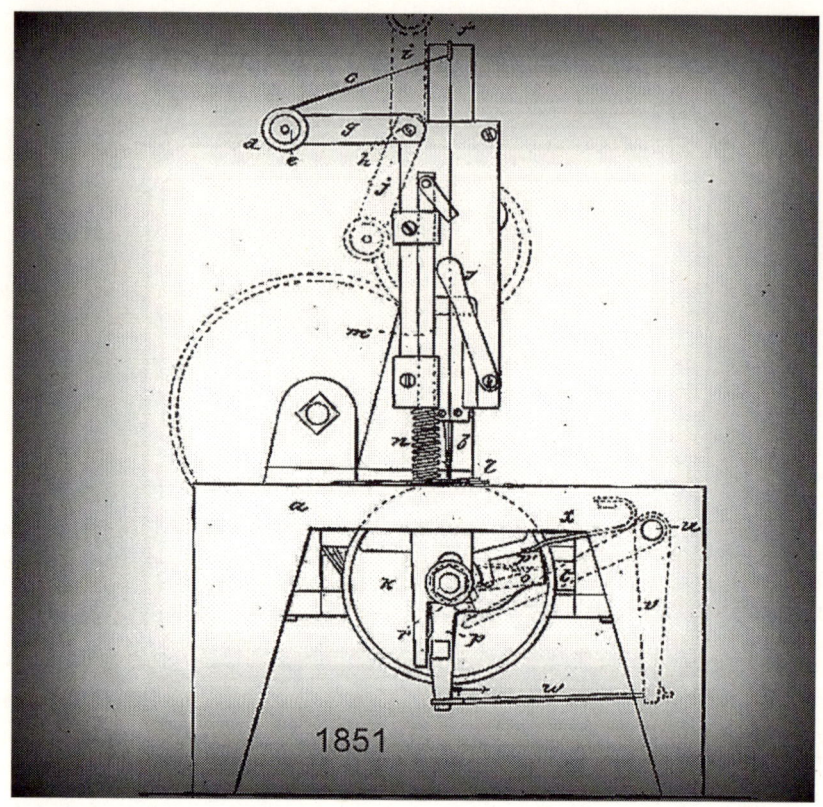

1851

The first realistic sewing machine in history was put together by Isaac Merritt Singer in eleven days flat. He patented it on 12th August 1851. His machine was reliable and factories soon started using it to increase their production. Isaac Singer went on to amass a great fortune, much of which he passed on to his countless children by several wives, mistresses, and lovers.

fortune suing everyone who used his patents. Eventually, Elias and the other big boys in the sewing industry got fed up with fighting each other and joined forces. They formed the illegal Sewing Machine Cartel and then sued everyone else. The Sewing Machine Cartel, Wheeler, Wilson, Singer, Grover, Baker and Howe all made a fortune suing and then selling licences to make sewing machines.

From this point in history sewing machines settled down and finally we come to the Great Exhibition in London in 1851, where Charles Judkins demonstrated the only British sewing machine. His power driven machine sewed nearly 500 stitches into fabric in one minute.

Time rolled on and as all the patents ran out, manufacturers would copy the best ideas without being sued and true mass production followed. The rest as they say is history.

By the late Victorian period the sewing machine had been hailed as the most useful invention of the 19th century releasing women from the drudgery of endless hours of sewing by hand. Factories sprung up all over the world to feed the insatiable demand for the sewing machine. Germany had over 300 factories alone. By the year 1900 over 20 million sewing machines a year were being made. It had become the biggest industry the world had ever seen.

By 1926 The American Patent Office (that had one sewing machine patent in 1842) had over 150,000 different patent models and millions of patents relating to sewing machines.

There is no doubt that Isaac Merritt Singer put together the first marketable sewing machine that was reliable, did what it was designed to do, and came with a guarantee that was worth the paper it was written on. His machine set the manufacturing world on fire and then spread from the factories to the homes until almost every household had the use of a sewing machine.

It is true to say that no single invention had ever been as eagerly accepted by people in all four corners of the planet as the humble, and often overlooked, sewing machine. It is one small machine that silently touches our daily lives and I expect that right now every single reader will be able to see something stitched on a sewing machine, even if they are sitting on it!

ONE OF THOSE DAYS

We all have bad days. You know the sort when the planets align to give you grief. One particular day it was happening to me by the bucket load, and right from my first appointment, I knew it was going to be a cracker, "Oh, it's not convenient now," said the first call of the morning as she shut the door in my face. I had called to set up her industrial machine and was spot on time. I stood staring at the brown oak door, which had been slammed in my face, wondering if she had misunderstood why I was there. But after running through the last moments in my mind I was sure that I had made myself perfectly clear. I pondered if she had thought just how much effort it takes to make sure that I arrive exactly as arranged, the early start, the time sitting in the ever growing traffic jams, even the cost of it all and the disruption to a carefully planned day, all to have the door slammed on me.

Oh well I thought, there is always McDonald's where a good cup of coffee can restore a dying man. I made a mental note to remember her for when she was desperate, as all professional seamstresses are at some point. It is one of the funny things about machinery, it always breaks down when you need it most, when it is under the maximum pressure. I shook my head and went for my cup of nectar.

After the necessary refuelling I made my way towards Eastbourne DGH and my next call at their linen room. On the way by Watts lane I notice Leonard Stevens bombing down the hill on his grey Dawes racing bike. Nothing unusual you may think, until I tell you that Leonard, who still runs the saddlery shop in Old Town with his wife, is over 90! Watts Lane has to be one of the steepest hills in town and I swear one day he will mistime his brakes and end up on the bonnet of a car along the main road that dissects the hill.

Later in the morning I was busily servicing the sewing machines in the linen department of Eastbourne District General Hospital. Everything was fine until I went to leave and found a penalty ticket on my car. Since my last visit, the place that I had parked in for over 20 years had been designated a no parking zone and a £70 fine was laughing at me from the other side of my windscreen. To make matters worse some idiot had parked behind me. As I manoeuvred out a crooked nosed old woman with a bad haircut and a nasty snarl started shouting at me out of a window across the yard. At first I guessed that she may have been an inmate of the psychiatric ward but as I wound down my window I caught the full brunt of her abuse being hurled at me and my parking in a no parking zone. I drove away from my onslaught with a few choice words of my own and wondered what the hospital management would think about her attack on an unsuspecting member of the public. They had enough problems with their public appeal without staff like her adding to them. Depressed, I moved on hoping for a better call.

It wasn't better. At Cavendish School I backed into one of the parent's cars as I tried to negotiate out of a tight spot. Next thing I knew there was a clonk and a cold feeling slid down me. Luckily it was the tiniest of dings but we all know what work on cars cost and later I found out to my dismay that 'clonk' was the sound of 230 pounds disappearing out of my bank account.

At the next call I passed through a spider's web and an enormous spider fell onto my face. Normally I'm fine with my eight legged friends but this one caught me by surprise. Screaming like a girl I dropped my toolbox and tried to brush away the web that had stuck to my face. While I was leaping around like a mad thing and flapping my jumper the huge monster dropped inside and onto my chest and then bit me! Spiders can't normally penetrate the skin with their tiny fangs but if they are big enough and have the added boost of my jumper crushing them, they can. It's nothing serious and usually disappears within a day or two. I did a pretty good impersonation of an Irish Jig and kept flapping my jumper and shirt until it fell out. It hit the pavement at full speed, scurrying away into the undergrowth. I looked down at my chest and saw a small red welt coming up. Just as I calmed down and pulled the last of the cobwebs from my face I looked up to see my customer's door move.

A tiny grey haired old dear was tugging away at her door as if she was opening the gates to a prison. Eventually it opened and she stood staring up at me in her yellow marigold gloves. "I wear these to stop me slipping over. I grip onto everything and pull myself around," she said as she showed me in. "The machine is upstairs if you would like to follow me." I noticed her husband sitting at his dining room table reading a paper. He made no acknowledgement of my arrival and just stared down at the daily news in front of him.

The old dear started her ascent of the stairs and I soon realised it was similar to climbing Everest. She gripped the hand rails on both sides and with a huge puff hoisted herself up each precarious step. Her marigolds squeaked in disproval as each one tightened around the rails. She sounded like she was strangling a hamster. Before long she had made it to the third step and I decided it was time to start following so I carefully moved up bit by bit. We were half way up the North Face, possibly the most difficult ascent in modern times, when her wheezing reached a crescendo. "I'm 93 you know," she gasped out between snorts. "I normally only come down in the morning and go back up to bed at night so this is an extra workout for me today."

After a short break we started again, the dark stairway seeming more precarious than ever as we neared a small landing, which turned at right angles and continued upward a few more steps to the bedrooms. Three clay ducks, pinned to the 70's flock wallpaper looked as if they were making a dash for safety. I knew we could have a breather once she made it to the landing, maybe even put up a base camp and let down ropes for our return journey. The top was in sight, but just as things were going splendidly, as with all the greatest challenges in life, disaster struck! The old dear grabbed the hand rails and heaved herself upwards with supreme effort, the gloves squeaking as her grip tightened and then, at the point of greatest strain, she did the most enormous fart! Being right behind her I had no warning and no chance of escape. I'm sure it blew a parting in my hair. Choking, I turned and made a run for it back down the stairs and into the living room. The old man looked up as I gasped for breath and he knew in an instant what had happened. "Mabel often drops her guts half way up," he said without missing a beat, "it's the strain you know. I should have warned you. She is 93! I always go to bed before her."

I waited for a while and went upstairs just as she turned on the light in the spare room. "I wondered where you had got to. Did you forget something?"

"No," I muttered trying to think on my feet. "I just wanted to see if your husband was okay." A lame excuse but far easier to explain than the real answer. She sat down next to the machine and stayed with me as I fixed it. "Would you like to go down first?" She asked as I finished. "You are quicker than me."

"Thanks," I replied as I ran for the stairs. In the living room I heard the squeaking marigolds getting closer and closer. When she came into the room she said, "Harold open the window dear, it seems a little stuffy down here." I almost burst out laughing. She paid and I left.

By late afternoon on my day of days I popped into T J Hughes in town to buy a new body warmer as I had lost mine the week before and for the life of me could not remember where. I would eventually get it back but as I had found out the last time I misplaced one, it may take a year before it turned up. I was just walking towards the paying area when a wide woman in a large checked coat sideswiped me and lumbered to the till, clutching a blue shirt. I sighed and patiently started a queue behind her.

"Look pet, I need a shirt for Jim, he's lost a lot of weight you see and he needs a new one. Not been well our Jim but he's over the worst now. Will this fit him?" The young lad serving behind the till was stumped for an answer but then came up with a solution. "I'll open it for you madam and you may be able to tell how large it is and if it might fit."

"Aye pet, right good idea." The shirt was duly unpacked and held out in front of the woman. She eyed it up and down, then made me jump out of my skin as she shouted, "STAN, STAN, WHERE ARE YOU, DAFT 'APETH? Ah, there you are," she said as she spotted him. "Will this fit Jim? You know he's lost a lot of weight since he's nought bin well"

"No," said Stan, who was leaning on his walking stick half way along the queue that had formed behind me. "We'll take it," she announced to a confused huddle of onlookers who were now queuing and being entertained as the little soap opera unfolded. "I've seen same on t'internet but this saves me trying t'fathom out how to order it." With the patience of a saint the confused shop assistant packed it up and made sure she had a gift receipt for when it was brought back. "COME ON STAN, WE'LL BE LATE FER COACH," she shouted as she manoeuvred magnificently by the shoe display towards the door. Sniggering, I paid for my body warmer and got to the exit just in time to see the old dear being manhandled by an eager driver onto a large white Shearings Holidays coach from Wigan. I took a deep breath and thought that life was not all bad and even better, I only had one more call in town and I would be done for the day.

I parked in Hartington Place for my last call, which turned out to be worse than the first of the day. I worked for over an hour on a Singer 280k, a complex machine built in the 1950's with two curved needles above and two loopers below, which caught the thread to form a stitch as it cut the edge of the fabric and joined it. In the end the old girl, which had not worked for over 10 years, just would not respond and failed to make a reasonable stitch even with all my best efforts. In my job my customers know that if I don't fix the machine perfectly then I don't charge and trying to fix her machine was like trying to tie up cobwebs. The machine was just too worn to respond, so I ended up not charging.

The day had been a total wipe out and I had probably lost the highest amount in any of my work days over the last 40 odd years. It was like one of those antiques programs off the telly where all the 'experts' buy goods and end up losing money on them at the auctions. It was very unusual for me but for every bad day I usually had countless crackers; you know the sort of thing, you turn up to do one machine and find six more waiting. At least I was finished and tomorrow was a whole new day of opportunities and potential earnings.

I came out of my customer's house and looked directly across the road at a pleasant three storey mock Georgian property, all brightly painted and shining in the afternoon sun. It was one of the most select addresses in town, number six Trinity Trees, which used to be part of Seaside Road. However as I stood staring at it a cold shiver went down my spine. The modernised property in the wide tree-lined street was where possibly one of the most prolific killers in British history lived, the infamous Bodkin Adams, or Doctor Death as the local kids called him. As I drove home memories of the little fat man with big hands and light feet came flooding back, for he was one of Eastbourne's most notorious residents.

The curtains are blowing in the cool night breeze, a doctor is kneeling next to the bed of his dying patient, praying as he helps her pass quietly out of this world into the next. He had opened the

Six Trinity Trees look harmless enough all freshly painted in the sunshine but as kids we would run by, what was a shabby old place, just in case Bodkin Adams was around. After his arrest many items were found in his basement, trophies, kept from his patients. Some of them went up for auction early in 2017 when the shop How We Lived Then, in Chiswick Place, was cleared out.

window to let her soul escape. It seems just like a scene out of a London theatre, but this is real. However there is a problem, a big problem, the version of events told by the respectable doctor Bodkin Adams before his trial for murder, differed dramatically to that of the only other witness, the maid, who had been silently shivering in the hall listening to what was going on in the bedroom. From the maid's statement, as her employer, Clara Neil Miller lay dying for the best part of an hour, she had been stripped. Her bedclothes had been thrown over the foot of the bed, and her nightgown had been pulled over her head. The only sounds coming from the room were the shallow breaths of Clara and the quiet murmurings of the Ulster doctor as he read from his worn bible. When Clara finally slipped away, the doctor quickly covered her, closed the window and left. It was contradicting statements like these (when his case came to trial) that set the media into a feeding frenzy.

There are few people who have caused such divided opinion in our town and even today there are still many people who knew him. Some loved him but just as many would never turn their backs on him.

As a young eager doctor, Dr John Bodkin Adams cycled into Eastbourne in 1922 to answer an advert placed in a paper looking for doctors to tend to a growing community of old patients. Who would ever guess that 35 years later that same man, now rich from bequests, would be standing in court charged with murder and to everyone's amazement, walked away a free man. They say that when Adams arrived in Eastbourne both the funeral directors and the crematorium prospered!

Although the police had investigated over 400 deaths that he was involved in, he was never convicted. As children we would run past his neglected old house, Kent Lodge, for we all knew if we were caught we would never be seen again. However it was not children who needed to be wary of Adams but the wealthy old 'Eastbourne Set' which even Adams admitted had more money than sense. Eastbourne was a rich picking ground for someone with the right character and the amiable smiling fat-faced Adams seemed to be the perfect doctor, with one exception, his patients kept dying!

Adams had a technique of isolating his wealthier patients and keeping them to himself and as his patients died his wealth grew. More strangely so did his collection of objects that he like to acquire from his dead patients. Many were the well-heeled elite of Eastbourne, including the 10th Duke of Devonshire, who was later named as one of his patients. When court cases were brought by grieving relatives written out of wills, Bodkin Adams would just explain that it would be impolite to refuse the bequests!

The trial of Bodkin Adams started at the Old Bailey the year I was born in 1957, and besides being the longest murder trial in British history up until that date, it was one of the most sensational trials of the century. His trial became a frenzy of reporting all across the world and it made the fat little doctor a macabre celebrity. It was extraordinary to arrest and prosecute a doctor, who was a leading member of the community and it was unheard of in the 1950's. As he was being led away from Kent Lodge, after his arrest, he grabbed his receptionist's wrist and whispered, "I'll see you in heaven."

Bodkin Adams was a comforting round faced man with a cheerful disposition. Many of his old patients, especially the women, adored him and would not hear a bad word said about him.

Although the detective in charge was quite sure Bodkin Adams was a mass murderer, any hard evidence was cleverly destroyed or hidden. There was enormous circumstantial evidence of his involvement in so many deaths, including being left countless gifts and being named in over 132 wills, but there was not one concrete piece of evidence strong enough to convict him of murder. "Murder, murder, can anyone prove murder?" Bodkin Adams would shout.

His defence team never let him take the stand, secretly telling colleagues that the greedy pig-headed fool would have soon hanged himself. Adams was found not guilty of murder. Back in 1957 had Bodkin Adams been found guilty of even one murder he probably would have been hung, so when he was found not guilty he openly wept in court. His humility was short-lived as within hours he was spotted having a slap-up meal.

Adams was subsequently found guilty on 13 lesser charges, including forging prescriptions, lying on cremation forms and obstructing the police. All-in-all he walked away with just a fine. Rich from countless bequests, the amount was easily paid.

On the plus side his trial triggered new stricter laws to keep better control of dangerous drugs.

Adams was struck off the medical register for a few years but had gained such enormous wealth from his patients it mattered little. Even the impressive 18 room Kent Lodge with its wonderful seaward views had been bought with money from one of his benefactors. As one reporter said, Bodkin Adams arrived in Eastbourne on a bicycle and now floats around in one of his chauffeur driven Rolls Royce's, incidentally left to him by another patient whose death was investigated!

Was Bodkin Adams a psychotic mass murderer? A true psychopath has no guilt and consequently feels no remorse. Because a psychopath feels no remorse they do not think that they have done anything wrong and consequently act like an innocent person. Adams, a member of the strict Plymouth Brethren, would have quite likely passed a lie detector test, for he believed that the Lord guided him in every way and how could that be wrong!

After the sudden demise of a patient the bumbling Adams instantly transformed into a model of proficiency and in no time at all he had often sorted out the funeral arrangements, including embalming, with his favourite undertakers. Most of his patients, except for a handful, were cremated, all apparently as they had wished. Statistically in that period burials were still very popular so the removal of evidence by cremation was ideal and the dead patient was not going to argue!

Julia Bradnum was one of the few who had left strict instructions to be buried. Once she was exhumed from the cemetery opposite what was the Girl's High School (now Cavendish School) in Eldon Road the doctor examining her found that she had not died from what Adams had put on the death certificate. When the police investigated further they found that the day before Adams visited she had been out walking and busying herself around her house. On the day of Adams' call he injected her and within a few minutes he announced that she was gone. He clipped his case closed and left.

His ability to charm his old clients was legendary, even holding bible classes at his surgery. In stark contrast was his hidden side, a true Jekyll and Hyde, his darker side hidden behind the happy bumbling act he put on. At a party no one guessed that the monster in the room was the fat cheeky doctor who loved the buffet. After his release he sold his version of events to a daily newspaper for £10,000 and when he died in 1983 the money was found untouched in an envelope among his artefacts.

Macabre as it seems, the large collection of trophies found in his basement obtained from his patients, were auctioned off to eager collectors at Edgar Horns in South Street. Some of them went up to the Towner Museum and Gallery in Gildredge Park where they were put on display for everyone to see. A few ended up in the brilliant shop and museum, How We Lived Then in Chiswick Place, run by Graham Upton and his wife, Jay. Graham is retiring soon and yet another great museum in Eastbourne will probably bite the dust.

As kids we didn't need facts; gossip was fine, like the stories of the bodies dug up for the trial in Ocklynge Cemetery or his love of cakes from Bondolfi's just along the road from his surgery. We knew that a smile from Bodkin Adams was dangerous but one day when I was about 10 he caught me staring at the cakes outside Bondolfi's coffee shop. I had cycled down from Stubberfields, the bike shop in South Street where I had just spent my last few pennies on two new brake blocks for my bike. On impulse I had decided to take a peek at the fabulous display that the cake shop would put on. I shot down South Street, past my doctors at The White House and did a squealing skid on the corner of the roundabout leaving a satisfying black rubber mark on the pavement. Well, I had to test my brakes didn't I? Jim Law who had just fitted the blocks back at the bike shop had done a great job.

Bondolfi's window was as stunning as ever with rows of Swiss pastries and delicacies from chocolates to cakes all displayed to delight the eye and all way too expensive for me; one cake would cost me a week's paper round money paid to me by my eldest brother for helping him every day. One day I must write the whole story of the Swiss patisserie, as it was the finest cake shop that Eastbourne has ever had.

There is little doubt that, to most of the older Eastbourne residents, Bondolfi's was the best patisserie we have ever had. Bondolfi lived just down the road from me on the corner of Ashburnham Road. One day I will write his story as it is a fascinating tale, including internment during WW2, whipped cream, and lashings of icing sugar.

Looking like the perfect street urchin in my oversized hand-me-downs I was dribbling at the delicacies on display when a shadow came over me and I looked up to see Dr Death himself smiling down. Adams was always immaculately dressed, usually in Savile Row suits, mainly black and usually sporting a chunky stubby hat. If you saw him once you never forgot him. Adams had a peculiar habit of folding up one pound notes into small squares and putting one into each of his pockets. I never found out why. He fiddled in one of his pockets and pulled out a note. With his huge hands he unfolded it and went into the shop. We did not exchange words but on his way out he tapped me on the shoulder and handed me a paper bag. Inside was a jam doughnut, the only delight that I had ever had from that magnificent shop.

That was the dilemma that the public had; he was half a cheery friendly charismatic chap and dedicated doctor who would help the poorest in society, and the other half was a quiet reserved man who had been caught manipulating old dears into changing their wills and, as the nurses testified, injecting them with his 'special' vitamins. Adams never made any qualms about his patients, "Easing the passing of a dying person is not all that wicked. She wanted to die. That can't be murder. It is impossible to accuse a doctor!"

Just above Bondolfi's in Cornfield Terrace was the Health Service Executive Trust where my friend, Pat Whippy worked. It was there in the 1960's that Adams was allotted his new patients when he got back his licence to practice.

One of my main hobbies as a kid was window-shopping, the perfect way to spend a few mindless hours planning what to spend my future millions on. The only other time I bumped into Adams I was doing just that. I was visiting another bike shop in town called Heaths Cycles in Cavendish Place. Horace Heath had a new range of Claud Butler bikes in and it was an opportunity not to be missed. I had been looking for another bike for my paper round and I could dream, couldn't I. A few doors along was P. J. Howes, where Cavendish Pharmacy is today. Phillip Howes was a chemist and in the 1960's when my friend Doreen Moore worked there, it was where Bodkin Adams would have some of his lighter prescriptions filled out. After his Trail he was banned from using the more dangerous drugs like heroine and morphine, and the ban was never lifted. His massive Rolls Royce silently slid to a halt on the kerb beside me and out popped Dr Death. He looked at me for a moment through his oval glasses, and then went into the chemist without a word. Although he was a short fat man he was really light on his toes and he almost skipped when he walked, which made him look even more peculiar. His cold clear stare had a piercing quality that made you freeze and as soon as he went inside I high-tailed it as quick as my little legs could pedal. I mean there was no chance of a doughnut from a chemist shop, was there!

By the time of his trial Bodkin Adams was a wealthy man and he had hired the best defence team in the country. They destroyed the prosecution time after time, pulling each individual piece of evidence to shreds. They successfully broke every chain of evidence and blamed sloppy nurses, poor paperwork and even worse record keeping but a true psychopath always prepares well and plays the part to perfection. In Bodkin Adams' case he was described as a cheery bumbling doctor who worked tirelessly to help the sick, often failing to keep records. Also, we all know that even today a good barrister can get away with murder.

Adams was a clever little man, it was written all over him but when it suited him he had perfected his bumbling routine. For his ageing flock, one of his little tricks was to fall to his knees before entering a patient's room and pray, making enough noise of course for the weak, dying patient to hear. Once he was caught red-handed in the act of changing a person's will. On that occasion his patient's wife overheard him instructing her husband on how to alter the will to leave everything to him. She burst in and found Adams clutching the will trying to help the man to sign. In a fury she chased him out of the house and had him banned from ever visiting again.

Did Dr Death get away with mass murder? A trial today may have had a very different outcome to the original but Adams walked out a free man and spent his final years reinstated as a doctor, and enjoying his hobbies, which included photography and his big love, shooting.

In a final twist of fate I once heard that when he was dying, after a hip operation at the our local hospital, in fear for his life, he refused the very pain killing drugs that he had administered to so many of his unsuspecting patients. How ironic.

A service was held for him at Holy Trinity Church just along the road from his house and where I had been married a few years earlier. It was once again a TV and media frenzy with the national press mingling in with the mourners to get a few juicy titbits. After he was cremated at Langney Cemetery, his ashes were taken to his parent's grave in Northern Ireland. Bodkin Adams died a wealthy man and in a final twist he left a nice settlement to every woman who testified for him at his trial.

We take the places we live for granted. Like so many towns, Eastbourne has a prim and proper surface but if you delve just a little deeper a fascinating dark world appears and none has a darker tale than Dr John Bodkin Adams. Was he a mass murderer or the perfect doctor? What do I know, I hardly knew the man.

THE END

East Sussex has to be one of the most beautiful places on earth when the sun is shining. Here is my wife Yana and daughter Sarah, with me at Birling Gap. The chalk cliffs known as the Seven Sisters are stretching out behind.

Bodiam Castle is on the edge of my area. Luckily for me it has great tea rooms so I just have to check them out when I am working nearby.

This stunning house in Ditchling is rumoured to have once been owned by Anne of Cleves and has had several famous inhabitants.

One of the most dramatic events that has happened in Eastbourne was the burning of Eastbourne Pier in July of 2014. I was in town when I saw the smoke and made my way up to the seafront to be confronted by a remarkable scene. The crowd were pushed back by police as the fire took hold and burned out of control. Due to the low tide and the pier structure it was near impossible for the firefighters to get at the heart of the inferno. By about six o'clock in the evening the fire had burned itself out but the Blue Room was completely destroyed.

Reconstruction of the pier started quickly thanks to Sheikh Abid Gulzar, who invested heavily in its reconstruction.

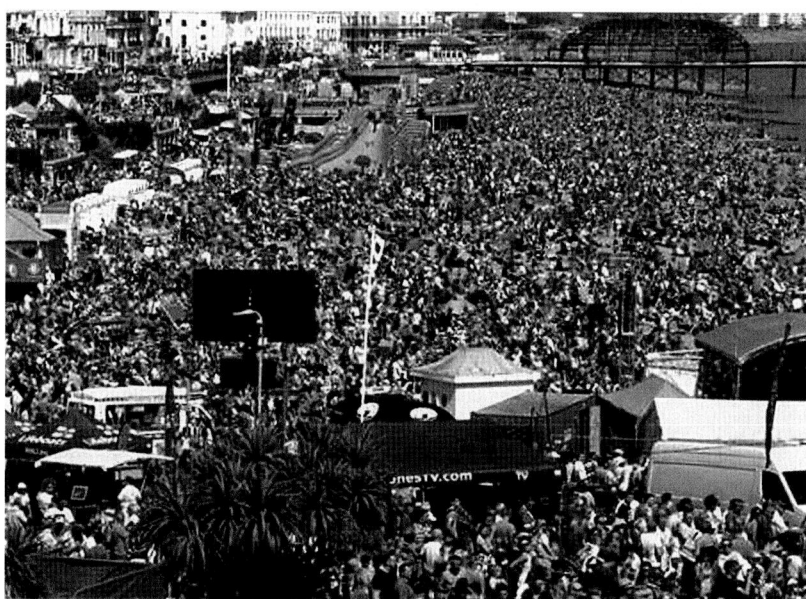

It is difficult to imagine how busy Eastbourne can get when an event like Airborne is on. There is hardly a space on the beach and the people look more like pebbles. Notice the burnt out pier.

Eastbourne was one of the most heavily bombed towns in the south during WW2, mainly due to being on the flight path to London. However, although we lost thousands of homes, many stunning properties survived. Eastbourne Town Hall and the properties surrounding it look impressive at any time of day.

Our earliest Bronze Age relatives lived and traded from these types of huts. This is a replica by Sevenoaks Road, part of Willingdon Levels which leads to west Langney, Shinewater & Hydney lakes. At sunset it is easy to step back in time there.

Roses in June
(Many thanks to Frank Richardson for the photos)

It was the first day of June and as I opened the door to leave for work I was hit by the wonderful scent of roses, hanging deliciously in the windless morning air. I surveyed my world, sniffed a few of them, smiled to myself and jumped into my beast. I flicked the ignition and rumbled up Church Street; my working day had begun. I only had three calls in the morning and the last one was to Frank Richardson, who it felt like I had known for a million years.

Since I was a kid in the 1960's, Frank had been driving around Eastbourne in a green Bedford flatbed van, identical to the one that me and my dad used to deliver sewing to our outworkers at Simplantex, the family business. Frank had a bric-a-brac store opposite Gore Park Road, by Donahue's the Butchers and Forbes the Chemist. I used to idly stare at his ever-changing display as I went by it most days on my walk to and from St Mary's School. Dad hated his Bedford van and one day on a back road from London it broke down for the last time. My dad stomped off to

Here is Frank and me with his precious Bedford van behind. I'm holding one of Frank's paintings (which I managed to get from him). It was a painting the he did of his old shop along Seaside where he sold his furniture and assorted oddments.

find a phone box as my mum and I waited for rescue. Hours went by before help arrived, then the van went one way and we went the other. I never saw it again. From then on Frank's was the only green Bedford in town. Over the years the van has become a bit of a celebrity in itself. His sons miraculously manage to keep it on the road for him.

I have worked for Frank for around 30 years. From his original shop he moved to another along Seaside then to Cavendish Place, before finally retiring and tinkering in a shed in his back garden. He has been married to his wife for over 67 years, as I mentioned earlier in the book he once told me his secret to a long marriage was painting. "When things get hot in the kitchen, I just get to my shed and paint! Works for me," Frank laughed.

Frank was always a mine of amazing information and to me he seemed timeless. He had not changed much since I could remember but had to be in his late eighties if a day. People had come and gone but Frank, like the pyramids, was always there and I was looking forward to his easy banter as I worked on his machine.

My first call of the day was to one of my regular customers, along a narrow road near the Territorial Army barracks along Seaside. The road does not have enough room for two cars to pass and often there is no parking so it can be a long walk getting to Bev's house with all my tools. Beverly runs a couture high fashion business called Sparkle Designs, specialising in ballroom and Latin dance dresses.

There was parking right outside her house so someone was smiling sweetly on me. I called and got down to work on the machines, which were completely fluffed up with assorted shiny bits, sequins, sparkles and fabric. All the paraphernalia that goes into world-class couture. Beverly has worked with several TV stars and one of my favourites was Jill Halfpenny who was on Strictly Come Dancing a few years back. In the first two series the costumes for the show were mainly made by a company called Chrisanne who Bev worked for. Jill Halfpenny was loaded with talent and within a few weeks we watched her progress right up to the finals where she won, with some fantastic dance routines, and jaw dropping dresses.

As usual I am digressing, so let me get back to my story. I have cans of compressed air to clean out the machines before I start to service and set them. One of the drawbacks of compressed air is that it blows the fluff everywhere and with Bev's machines being full of sparkles, after an hour of work I was covered in an assortment of glittery things.

As I left Bev's I walked out into Cambridge Road. The terraced houses have small front gardens so you almost step straight out onto the pavement. In the sunshine I looked down at my clothes and noticed I was sparkling worse than a contestant in one of Bev's competitions. I put my toolbox down and brushed myself off as best as I could. As all the glittery bits flew from my clothes they drifted in the light wind and caught the sunshine, sparkling like floating Christmas decorations. For a moment I was transfixed by the sight. There was an old man walking along and as he passed I nodded to him and said with a smile, "Morning." He looked me up and down with a face that would sink a lifeboat and went on his way, muttering to himself something about Eastbourne turning into Brighton and now being full of weirdos! Ah, another work day in Eastbourne, I thought. Bev came out to tell me that I still had dress sparkles all over my face. She brushed me off as I chucked my tools into the back of my old banger.

"How many sugars did you just put in your tea, Vicky?" I asked Victoria in astonishment. I had been watching her closely and after the third spoonful, I was wondering if she was losing her marbles. I was about to get a lesson in minding my own business!

"Four and a half teaspoons. Why?"

"Oh, it just caught me by surprise I thought my two spoons 'builders tea' was a lot."

"Oh no, four and a half is just right for me. I find five a little too sweet. It's a miracle food, sugar."

"How do you figure that then?"

"Oh don't believe all that malarkey so-called experts spout at you today. Some may be true but most of them are passing fads: Don't eat butter, don't eat eggs, carbohydrates kill! Drink eight pints of water a day, whatever next. Fish don't even drink that much! My mother was born on 22 June 1887 on the day of Queen Victoria's Golden Jubilee. She named me after her when I turned up as a surprise gift in 1930 when she was 43 years old. She lived until she was 93 and the only time she was rushed into hospital, the first thing they did was put her on a saline drip and take her blood sugar to see if it was low! She only died after a fall.

Mother loved sugar and so do I, and just about every other living creature from bears to bees love it too. All this rubbish about it being bad for you, pah! If you look at it, there is sugar in every ripe piece of fruit and lots of it, long before we figured out how to refine sugar cane and sugar beet, which are grass and vegetables I might add, there were plenty of fat people around. You only have to look at a few portraits in the National Gallery to see some of them and they never had a spoonful of sugar in their lives. Today all these experts say 'don't eat this, don't eat that', most of these so-called experts are probably being paid by the huge food firms messing around with our crops and creating 'Frankenstein Foods' for the future.

I tell you I went out with Betty to The Hydro last week for afternoon tea. As she was popping pills into her drink she had explained very seriously how she can't eat sugar anymore because she's 'type two' you know! Then she went on to have two slices of cake! Apparently the highest consumption of sugar in the world is Asia and yet they have one of the lowest records of obesity. How do you explain that eh? And another thing, when I asked my old doctor the difference between the 'evil' sugar and that miracle food honey he laughed and said they are the same but one has the added ingredient of bee sick! When rationing of sugar came to an end, around 1953, we used to almost fill our mugs with it when we made tea. After we had supped all the tea, we would spoon out the bottom of the sticky cups for our pudding. I know that was a bit extreme but we hadn't seen sugar for years, so we went a bit mad.

I would love to know who 'they' are, filling youngsters full of artificial flavourings, E-numbers and preservatives. God only knows how long they will live on the modern junk food that is so full of flavourings and additives that there is no room for real food. The experts should be looking at our generation and why we have lived so long compared to everyone before us. Do you know what we used to eat?"

"No Vicky but I have the feeling I am just about to find out." We both laughed. I would have loved to find a soap box for her to stand on. Vicky was coming to the boil and continued with her rant. "Ten portions of fruit and veg a day. How ridiculous! The only fruit I saw most of the year was in my Christmas stocking. Breakfast was milk and bread, lunch suet with fatty bacon or tripe or fish. Supper would be something like real ox tail soup or soup from cow heels, with more bread and salt. Salt with almost everything, we even put it on a rag and brushed our teeth with it.

If I find out who these so called experts are I'm going to whack them with my handbag. I might even put a brick in it! During World War Two the buses went round with huge adverts on the sides, 'Eat bread for energy'. Also, I almost lived on fish and chips back then, that and dripping. You know the cold fat and juices left in the bottom of the roasting pan. We would spread it on toast and sprinkle it with, you guessed it, salt! Uncle George had a chip shop and neither fish nor potatoes were rationed, so I ate them at least four times a week. And what's more," said Vicky who was quite red-faced now as her rant continued, "Uncle George used to fry his chips in pure lard. Can you believe it! They tell youngsters today if they even sniff lard they'll be dead by the weekend."

"Well Vicky," I said laughing. "I think you have just made my day."

"Oh it's not for everyone mind, especially if there is a medical reason, but sugar is my little miracle."

"But what does your doctor say?"

"What does my doctor say? I have outlived four of my doctors, all of whom tried to make me cut down, so I'll carry on a while longer. A little bit of what you fancy don't do you no harm." We both giggled. "Now let me stir your troubles for you," she added swishing her spoon around my coffee cup. I took a sip wondering for the first time what it would taste like with double the sugar!

After my wonderful call to Vicky at East Dean I dropped down the Jevington Road towards Polegate, where Frank lived. The road was smooth and dry. As I rolled by the edge of Friston Forest, two buzzards were circling lazily above the forest using just the odd wingbeat when they turned on the thermals. June was busting out all over and the fields were a blaze of colour. The fields disappeared as I drove through a deep canopy of trees just before the small hamlet of Jevington.

I passed the Hungry Monk, which was once the finest dining establishment in the area but has now been converted back into

The Hungry Monk cottages were once the home of the finest dining place in our area. The only indication left now is the plaque on the cottage wall mentioning Banoffi Pie.

cottages. Looking, I imagine, much like their 17th century originals. From 1968 the restaurant was run by Nigel Mackenzie and he had the magic touch with his food, and his customers. Over the years I had dined in his restaurant a few times and also met some of his staff; one was a cook, whose sewing machine I had fixed and another who was working at John Barkworth's, an Osteopaths in College Road that I visited regularly, with my crook back. She had a part time job in the clinic during the day and worked as a waitress at The Hungry Monk in the evenings. Over the years they had all told me the same story of how Nigel had invented the world famous Banoffi Pie. The restaurant is now long gone but Banoffi pie will probably last forever and it all started at the little flint cottage in Jevington.

Banoffi Pie is now so famous that even Nestle print the recipe on the side of their condensed milk tins, and Haagen-Dazs makes a Banoffi Pie flavoured ice-cream. Apparently Nigel and his head chef Ian were playing with an old American recipe called something like 'coffee toffee pie', which was made with a can of boiled condensed milk. After the restaurant had closed for the evening, when things had died down, they tried different combinations of ingredients and fruits until Nigel added bananas to his toffee and biscuit recipe. The rest, as they say, is history, and hanging around the waistlines of the world! Before long they had come up with the simple name of Banoffi Pie. The pudding was such a great hit with the customers that people kept asking for the recipe and customers even booked their pudding when they booked their tables. Nigel had made something that, although simple in its ingredients, was just about perfect. As fame grew for his pie there was talk that other people had invented it before Nigel. At one point Nigel was said to have offered a reward of over £10,000 for any person who could prove the existence of a Banoffi pie before his invention in 1971. No one ever came forward to claim it and so a blue plaque was proudly placed on the wall of the Hungry Monk as a lasting reminder to one of the best restaurants, and puddings, we have ever had.

I rolled on down to Frank's house and found him pottering in his rambling back garden, pruning his roses. "Smell this one boy, it smells of heaven." Frank was right, in the morning sunshine the roses were putting on their best show and smelling just about perfect. A beekeeper once told me that flowers, especially roses, let their scent out around midday, the best time for maximum pollination and when the bees are most active. As we walked by one of Frank's sheds, towards where he kept his old sewing machine, I noticed a new painting of an aircraft carrier on his easel. "Working on a new painting, Frank?"
"That was the ship I went to war on."
"It's a whopper."

HMS Victorious was built at the Vickers-Armstrong shipyards at Newcastle-Upon-Tyne in 1937 and launched in 1939. From 1941 she saw some furious action including against the battleship Bismark. Her duties included several Artic Convoys and the difficult Pedestal Convoy to Malta. By late 1945 she was being used to carry servicemen to the Far East and pick up war brides from Ceylon and Australia.

"Nothing bigger in the British Fleet, Alex. It was the aircraft carrier HMS Victorious; pride of the Navy."

While I worked on Frank's Singer, out came a great story from days long past, one man's war with no one to fight!

Frank left school at 14 and went to work at Lacey's, Brighton's premier shoemaker in Trafalgar Street. Lacey's, opposite Freddie Rowe the butcher, made shoes for kids right up to size 14 for adults. Frank started his apprenticeship in 1941, when a pair of black leather handmade shoes cost eight shillings and eleven pence. I wonder how much a pair of made-to-measure leather shoes would cost today! I doubt if you would get change out of a few hundred quid. Rationing was in full force and only 10 pairs of leather shoes were allowed to be sold a day, but they could sell as many wellington boots as they liked. The result was that during World War Two there were loads more people walking around in wellies!

Queues formed daily before the shop opened in the chance of getting a well-made pair of Lacey's shoes. Strangely, because rationing made spending money quite difficult, people would spend more on the things that they could buy, like handmade shoes, so the shop prospered.

Poorer families could apply to the council for a 'boot voucher' for their children. If you were lucky enough to get a voucher, Lacey's was the best place to exchange it for boots. Only a limited number of youngsters were given boots each day so orderly lines formed with kids clutching their voucher. Eight boys at a time were allowed into the shop. They were then taken to the top floor where rows of hobnail boots, all identical, except for size, were hanging in sized rows. Once the correct boot size was found, steel toecaps were fitted and nails were hammered around the toe area. Then steel pelts were pinned into the heel. All this was done to make the boots last as long as possible, but this extra metal had other benefits, as we will soon find out.

One final task was carried out before the kids left, the boots were 'holed'. On the way out, each boy handed over his prized pair of hobnailed boots and had a hole punched out of the side, and the back, to show that they were 'free boots'. This was to stop desperate parents pawning them down the pawnbrokers once their kids brought them home!

The idea of all the protective steel on the boots backfired as the lads loved the hobnails, caps and pelts. They made the shoes slide as if on ice. Kids could skid all over the place, showing off their new shoes. They also made a right clatter as they walked and if they got it just right people could hear them coming from a hundred yards away. Even better, if you were lucky, on the right ground you could get a spark out of them! At the local schools they even made up games for the sliding. One was to hold hands and form a line. The line would start to turn in a huge circle. One by one, the boys were spun faster and faster. Each boy on the end of the line would judge the perfect time to let go and then slide across the playground. Whoever managed to slide closest to the school wall was the winner. This led to lots of scrapes and bruises but the lads loved it.

After a few years, with the war raging and Frank getting older he was as keen as mustard to sign up and join in. During World War

Two, Brighton was a hub of activity and Frank enviously watched the men and women from the armed forces move around the town. The railway station was always the centre of all the action and it became a meeting and parting place for many wartime romances. There was a large naval presence in Brighton with a naval training academy at Lancing College known as a Concrete Carrier, because it was based on land, not water.

One day Frank was outside his shop having a cigarette when his boss came out and started shouting at him. That was all the trigger Frank needed. He stubbed out his ciggy, marched up to the enrolment office and put his name down, enlisting on the spot.

That evening Frank wondered if he had done the right thing and decided that he would swallow his pride and try and get his job back in the morning. Being only 17 he thought they would not really bother with him until he was 18 anyway. How wrong he was. The next morning, on the doorstep with the 7am mail, was a letter asking Frank to report back to the enrolment offices to officially enlist. It was 1944 and the Allies were on the offensive to beat Hitler. The armed forces needed all the young men they could get.

Frank had voluntarily enlisted so they allowed him to take his pick of the armed forces. Frank hated the idea of having to bayonet anyone and decided to plump for the Navy. At his enrolment he was given several tasks to perform and a rigorous fitness inspection. All went well until Frank was asked to look at some cards, "What's on this card, boy?"
"Nothing, Sir."

"SPEAK UP, BOY."

"NOTHING, SIR."

"This card?"

"NOTHING, SIR."

"And this card?"

"THERE IS NOTHING ON THAT CARD, SIR."

"Son – you're colour blind."

"TELL ME SOMETHING I DON'T KNOW, SIR."

"Well, I'll tell you this, you're no sailor."

"I didn't join to be a sailor sir. There must be other jobs in the Navy that don't need all these colours. What about booking, Sir?"

"BOOKEEPING! WE DON'T NEED BOOKEEPERS. What did you do on civvy street boy?"

"I worked at a shop in Brighton sir."

"Well now there's a thing. We've been looking for you."

"What, sir?"

"We've been looking for someone to help run stores on the base at Portsmouth and it looks like we've just found him. THAT SUIT YOU, BOY?"

"YES SIR, SUITS ME FINE, SIR."

And so Frank was trained in the largely overlooked but essential job of store man for Naval Supplies at Portsmouth. Most of the bombing raids had stopped by then and his job in the stores was split between six others; three in mechanical supplies and three in the food division. Frank, along with a few other lads and a Petty Officer (who hardly ever showed up) had the best job in the Navy. He was almost self-employed; even the officers never upset him as he had control of the booze. He spent his days dishing out rations, stocktaking and wandering around the barracks. Sometimes on sunny days Frank would sweep the yard at a nice easy pace, get a tan, and chase off any scroungers who were after free rations.

One of the big bonuses of Frank's job was the rum rations! Rum rations were dished out daily and it was 80% pure alcohol. Unfortunately for Frank he was still only 17, meaning that his ration was milk, so he had to come up with a solution for this annoying problem! Although rum was closely guarded and rationing took place under the watchful eye of the duty officers, Frank soon came up with a cunning plan.

After the rum was poured from the barrels marked SRD, (Service Ration Depot) Frank then had to drain the last dregs of the empty barrels down the sink. They were drained so as to avoid any unpleasantness amongst the naval boys trying to get the last drips from them. The barrels were designed to empty completely when turned upside down. Each one was left over a large sink until the last drop had come out. Only then would the duty officer sign off and leave. It was while watching this hideous waste with a tear in his young eye, Frank came up with his idea.

For a split of 'the profits', Frank talked one of the base plumbers into modifying the sink drain traps so that any surplus went down the plughole, but then into a bucket hidden in a cabinet below. The very next evening they carried out their usual rum ration duties and as soon as the officer left they excitedly opened up the sink cabinet. Their plan had worked like a dream and nearly half a pint of rum was carefully shared out between them. During all the times that rum rations were served in their camp they were never caught.

Eventually Frank was moved to an overflow camp at Havant near Portsmouth for the final thrust against the Germans. However, just before he sailed, the enemy gave up. Frank always told me that the Germans had heard that he was coming and surrendered!

Victory in Europe Day was celebrated at the barracks with an enormous bonfire on the parade ground and a piano banging out tunes late into the night. Around Portsmouth the pubs were so heaving that not enough pint glasses could be found to keep all the sailors watered. In the harbour all the ships hooted and tooted and the sounds echoed around the bases in blasts of victorious noise. When one of the happiest of days came to an end and the men finally went to bed, they threw the piano onto the fire and laughed themselves to sleep.

Towards the end of the war there was a massive push towards the Far East to finish off the Japanese and Frank found himself on board H.M.S. Victorious, an aircraft carrier heading south with Task Force 37.

However the war took a turn for the better and on the 15th August 1945 the Admiralty contacted all British ships with wonderful news and instructions to 'splice the main brace', a code for a 'liquid celebration'. Basically drinks all round! It was the Admiralty's way of letting the ships in the fleet know that the Japanese had finally given up. The war was over. Frank found out when one of his shipmates shouted over to him, "Hey Frank, the Japs have heard you're coming!"
"How d'ya know?"
"They've surrendered!"

H.M.S. Victorious then received orders to divert to Sydney, Australia. On the way instructions came through to convert the warship into a troop carrier to get all the lads back to 'Blighty'. During this period an amazing thing took place on board the ship. There was now no need for most of the brand new Spitfires, Seafires and Hurricanes being carried to the Far East to help with the war effort. What they needed was space. As the ship cruised along, several planes (which had been lashed down to the flight deck) were unstrapped and shoved into the Indian Ocean. Then the crated planes below deck were lifted out and all through the night, one by one, heaved over the side. By the time they reached port their priceless cargo was at the bottom of the ocean. It is probably still there to this day!

Finally Frank ended up at a Royal Naval commando and fighter plane training base, HMS Nabstock, in Australia, about 60 miles outside Sydney. Here he spent his final months of the war, once again looking after the food and rum rations in the stores. As Frank was not under any particular command he could come and go pretty much as he pleased, so rather than stay at the half-deserted barracks he found a nice home and family to stay with a few stops down the train line. They had advertised for British Forces troops because if you put up any troops you received a payment. Frank quickly adopted his surrogate parents, even referring to them as 'Mum and Dad'. In his spare time he repaired their home and generally helped out around the place. With servicemen being constantly shipped back to Britain from all over the world, the base eventually emptied out and slowly closed down. Frank shut up shop and prepared to leave for England.

Stores staff at HMS Nabstock shortly before its closure.

By spring of 1946 the last remaining squadron, 706 Squadron, was disbanded and HMS Nabstock became a ghost camp. Frank was one of the last servicemen out of the huge base (which apparently remained empty for decades after). One day the last few men simply locked the gates and left the place to the wind and the wildlife.

At Darling Harbour in Sydney they all hopped aboard a banana boat called The Highland Princess. Darling Harbour was pandemonium. Thousands of people were seeing off the sailors and troops, possibly for the last time. The ship was covered in streamers and on the dockside a band was playing. The carnival atmosphere was suddenly broken when the ships whistle blasted. Everyone thought it was the sign for the ship to depart. Hundreds of screaming women broke through the barriers and made a rush for the ship. The lads were hanging over the side of the ship, the

The Highland Princess about to leave Darling Harbour for Perth. This is one of those superb iconic war photographs. Frank is in the top left corner as another sailor grabs one last kiss from his girlfriend. Who could tell if they would ever see each other again?

girls being lifted up for one last kiss before departure. General mayhem ensued before the ship finally pulled out of port just after noon.

Before departure the captain of the Highland Princess had turned off the coolers in the banana storage departments and the troops put their bunks up in the storage hold. However the insulated banana storage became unbearably hot and the crossing along

The Highland Princess was built by Harland & Wolff in Belfast for the Nelson Line in 1929. She passed to the Royal Mail for services in 1932 but by 1939 she was being used for troop duties. She was a 14,100 ton steel screw motor ship, 14,500 tons gross. The Highland Princess saw service all over the world from Argentina to Australia. Although only designed to carry a maximum of 400 passengers and personnel by the time troops were being shipped home over 800 were sometimes jammed on board.

the south coast to Perth was suffocating.

To keep cool after dark some of the men used to sneak up on deck and tie up their hammocks between the railings, sleeping like babies in the cool night air. They would sleep under the stars rather than try and stick out the suffocating heat below. One night a storm erupted and the men woke to find themselves locked outside in the middle of a thundering squall. Not knowing that Frank and his mates were sleeping on deck, the ship had been braced for the storm. All the hatches were battened down and the doors locked. In sheer panic, while hanging on to the ship as it tossed and turned, the lads tried all the doors. In the pitch-black rolling sea no one could hear their cries over the storm. Frank and the lads had to think quickly to survive. They grabbed all the rope they could find and lashed each other to anything solid and rode out the storm. At one point the bow of the ship was lifting out of the waves, as it crashed down the stern would heave up and the propellers would clear the water, screaming as they came out, then shuddering down again into the sea. After what seemed like a lifetime the squall subsided. All the lads luckily got through that long night. In the morning they untied themselves and fell exhausted to the deck. From then on, however hot, they slept back in the storage holds.

The Captain had been trouble from the start. He had not been happy about having to give up his valuable cargo space to servicemen. He had given orders for the troops to be fed on only the cheapest haricot beans, three times a day! This animosity was further fuelled because, although it was a banana boat it was quite luxurious, carrying fee-paying passengers to exotic destinations. The servicemen could clearly see the passengers eating like royalty.

It was not long before the troops rebelled against their unfair treatment in the hold. At one point one of the officers barely escaped up the ladder from the storage compartment where the angry men were billeted. He was being chased by some very upset and windy sailors! In a fury the Captain ordered the doors locked and the lights turned out. After a few hours in the black box the men calmed down and the minor mutiny was averted. The Captain then turned the lights back on. The men never trusted him again; even though he added a few over ripe black bananas to their 'bean' diet.

As the ship drew near to Fremantle Docks near Perth, news came that a huge parade was being put together on June 10, to celebrate the final end to hostilities. They needed all the armed forces to be represented. Nearly all the British boats had already left. Frank, being one of the last of the sailors, along with 30 others, led the parade along the streets of Perth just behind the Western Command Band banging out patriotic tunes.

Perth held the largest parade it had ever seen with over 100,000 spectators lining the streets. At the front of the 6,700 people who took part in the parade was Frank and his shipmates, proudly representing Britain and the armed forces. It became known as The Great Parade and one of the finest days in the city's history. Streamers flew, bunting blew and confetti drifted in the breeze as 12 bands played along the streets in a stunning spectacle. It was not all plain sailing for the men. The bad sea voyage from Sydney had left them with shaky legs. As the procession neared the centre of the parade, where the officials were, they stiffened up, grabbed the man in front of them by the shoulder, locked their positions and marched as one. As their Officer shouted "EYES LEFT," they all luckily looked right, where Lieutenant Governor Sir James Mitchell and his Wife were standing.

Celebrations carried on late into the night with torchlight processions but although the men were granted the freedom of the city, the Captain had stuck his oar in once again and told the officials that there might be trouble with Frank and the lads. As soon as the parade was over the men were whisked out of the town by lorries to a pub where free drinks were served, and where it didn't matter if a brawl or two broke out!

Back at Freemantle Docks the Captain was on them again. As they were about to board the ship, over the ship's tannoy came an announcement that the men would be searched for booze. Any found would be confiscated and the men punished. Before the inspection crew could get down the gangplank, to carry out their search, Frank and the lads swigged down every drop they were carrying. The crew couldn't do anything except help the cheering men back on board!

Frank stopped off in Colombo, Ceylon and worked in the stores once more, then to Singapore on board a new American ship that had been made after Pearl Harbour. Frank had time to rest there. In the dry dock was a huge Japanese warship that the Japs had sunk in the worst position rather than let the enemy get hold of it. When it was re-floated to get it out of the way, they found Japanese bodies inside, men that had apparently decided to go down with their ship rather than surrender! They towed the ship into the Johor Strait between Singapore and Malaya and sunk it again.

There were many incidents like this at the end of Frank's war. Another that stood out was when the American ship pulled out for the last time. It was showing off and moving too fast. It scraped the side of the dock and damaged a propeller but just carried on at full steam, leaving a trail of black smoke all the way to the horizon. Luckily the war was over as it would have been spotted from miles away by the enemy. Another was when Frank was in charge of stores tidying under a bench. Frank heard a voice, "I need some boxes for a show we are putting on." Frank was quick to react; his job was to keep scroungers out of stores and his stock correct. "Well you know what you can do. B*****

off and don't come back!" Frank stood up to see the base commander standing there in full uniform covered in scrambled egg (military in insignia). "I'm so sorry sir."
"Nothing to say sorry for son. Good job, well done. Now get the boxes delivered to the stage, soon as."

Frank returned to England on the sister ship to HMS Victorious, for demob. The ship was in poor condition after sustaining sever battle damage. She was almost on her final voyage before the scrapyard. During the crossing the back hangar of the rusting hulk was transformed into a cinema to entertain the returning troops. The front hangar was used for bunks, six high, and the canteen. Everything was fine until they hit a squall in the Mediterranean. They had already lost a propeller in the Indian Ocean so they were in no condition to ride out the weather. Everyone just held on as all the bunks went one way and the tables the other. Water poured in through the open hangars. Like a washing machine, the men, tables, food and beds all mixed together. Eventually the squall subsided and soaked they limbered on to Portsmouth.

At the docks Frank went for demob but found the offices had filed his paperwork months ago and had no current records for him. Frank scratched his head, collected his gear and walked off the base. His war was over without a single shot fired in anger. To his amazement, years later, when the Suez Crisis was on Frank received a letter from the Admiralty to tell him to be prepared to resume services. It turned out that he had never been officially demobbed!

Back home with mum and dad Frank went to work at Barratt's

Shoes in Brighton. Barratt's were one of the country's leading shoe retailers and are still in business today. Starting in Northampton just after the turn of the last century, they led the way with fashionable high quality footwear. Their slogan was 'Walk the Barratt Way'. Frank's experience at Lacey's and his store duties during the war made him the perfect applicant for the country-wide shoe retailer.

Before long Frank had been promoted to store manager, standing in for other managers around the country when they had their holidays. Eventually he managed his own Barratt's store in Dover before moving to run Barratt's in Eastbourne complete with seven girls and a foot X-Ray machine! Luckily for Frank, he refused to use the weird contraption, even when Norman Barratt came to see why. It wasn't because Frank knew the dangers of X-Rays, no one did then, but as Frank told his boss, "If we can't measure feet without that contraption, we're in the wrong job!" Norman Barratt left and took the machine with him to another store. That was slightly annoying as at Christmas the staff would put their presents under the machine. The X-Rays could see straight through the wrapping and show them what they had got! A while later, when the dangers of radiation were better known, all the machines were banned.

Before Frank had enlisted in the Navy he had met his one true love at a dance. She only lived just down the road from him in Brighton but when Frank was whisked away to Australia he did not have the opportunity to even say goodbye to her. "When your country calls you don't get time to think and no time for goodbyes either." When Frank returned from his war duties, back to life in 'Civvy Street', he mistakenly believed that she would never forgive him, or even talk to him again.

Frank would often see her on his way to work but could never build up the courage to talk to her until one day in June when he saw her in the park. With his heart pounding like crazy he picked a rose and asked her to forgive him. They chatted away for hours as if he had never been away. As they departed they made plans for a date. Sixty seven years later Frank and his wife are still together.

I left Frank working on his painting in his shed by his roses and made my way home for lunch. Once more Frank had bewitched me with his wonderful tales and once more I sucked them up like a new vacuum cleaner, loving every word.

Nigel Mackenzie passed away in July 2015 and is hopefully entertaining God with his delicious cooking and amazing Banoffi Pie. Let's hope he doesn't put on weight.

My Little Window
That Overlooks The Sea

A late summer wind rushed into my bedroom, brushing over me, dropping the warm sweet scents of night onto my face. It was excited and called to me in the midnight hour. Ever the insomniac I slipped quietly out of bed and crept to the window, leaned against the frame and stared out at the diamond filled sky. I rubbed my sleepy eyes and smiled at a scene which I had seen so many times before but was always breathtaking.

Eastbourne stretched out in front of me beneath a deep blue heaven. Countless yellow and white street lamps speckled the darkness like exploding sky rockets nailed to the ground. In the far distance, sweeping across the bay, was Hastings, its promenade party lights still inviting revellers.

In the countryside clumps of lights sparkled from the villages that were hidden in the comforting folds of the black Sussex earth. There was a full moon which made the sea shine like hammered silver; a passenger jet was flying in front of it and I was reminded of the scene from ET where the alien flies away on a bicycle and millions of children around the world shed tears for a small, imaginary creature.

The breeze from the warm southern lands of the continent engulfed me with exotic scents of earth and sea. Only hours before it would have been tumbling over the grain fields and ripe vineyards of France, then across the shadowy dark waters of the Channel to find our English soil.

In the hollows of the valley along Pigs Lane and Shinewater a low mist was forming and through the darkness the last of the herring gulls were making their way back to the seafront for the night. They would sleep safely on the sea before returning to some town, farmer's field, or rubbish tip at the next sunrise.

A bat flitted around our apple tree, picking off insects in the moonlight and a young fox sat by the pampas grass in our neighbour's garden. Foxes seem to love pampas grass and often play in and around it for hours. Its silhouette was lit up by a security lamp and I could see its pointed ears outlined like the silver lining on a cloud.

Down across the valley a four-carriage train was heading out of Eastbourne, curving along towards Normans Bay, its metallic whine cutting through the night air. It disappeared between the houses only to reappear a mile or so out of town. Its wheels sparked on the curve at Westham and then I lost it to the darkness. A lorry was hammering along the bypass, its red sidelights clearly visible as it raced through the night. The last bus was making its way down Maywood Avenue, its rear brake lights flashing back at an empty road as it pulled up at the junction of

Hazelewood.

I rubbed my sleepy eyes once more and surveyed my lands. In my mind, no more beautiful sight existed than this scene before me.

A long time ago, when I was just a nipper, my mum gave me a piece of priceless advice; always buy a house on a hill. How right she was, for I had spent decades being enchanted by my view and never grew tired of it.

I have always been captivated by the passing of time, but also jealous of how the world renewed itself each day, how time means nothing to this old earth as she hurtles through the endless void of space, this complicated and amazing world, where we mortals grow so quickly, rush headlong into our prime, and then cling to our old age in no more than a blink of an eye.

I turned my back on the moon, the stars, and the night, gently lay back down next to my sleeping wife and slept like a newborn baby.

The next morning I awoke and the world was grey. Rain had sneaked through the sleeping hours and stolen our lovely blue skies. It was early September and autumn was turning. A cold north wind had swept down the country, pushing showers down to the last tip of England. The best summers for 30 years had finally broken. I smiled to myself, because earlier in the night, the wind had called to me and stars from the Arabian Nights had sprinkled a bit of magic through my window, my little window that overlooks the sea.

Autumn in the Air

The quiet hush of early morning was broken by autumn being noisily announced. High on the North Wind came the excited claxon calls of geese, their cries tumbling down from the troubled sky. This was no warm seaborne breeze from southern climes they beat their wings upon, this was the cold wind of ice and storm, grown in the land of the midnight sun. It froze the warm necks of children hurrying to school and old ladies waiting for town buses; it chased litter and leaves, rounding them up in sheltered corners like some invisible road sweeper. The season of chills and frost was on its way and for the first time in many months, I shivered.

My first call of the day was to a retired school teacher, Marie Bartholomew. Marie had been going to patchwork classes and (much to my delight) had messed up her Bernina. Before long I was ploughing my way through the machine with Marie watching closely by my side. On her bookshelf were several of Virginia Woolf's books. "I have never really got into her books," I said, nodding towards the shelf.

"Oh, nor have I," replied Marie, "But I keep them as a memory of my childhood."

"How do you mean?"

"My father, Percy used to work for the Woolf's, and we lived in one of their cottages on the Rodmell Estate next to Monks House."

"Get away," I said, "That must have been an interesting childhood!"

"Oh, you have no idea. The Woolf's had two cottages besides their own house and we lived in one, my dad was the gardener and spent many hours chatting to them as he worked. They seemed to love his relaxed life and he enjoyed their company just as much. They had a place in London but that got bombed so they had decided to spend the war down at their holiday retreat. Virginia was an awful worrier, she used to get so upset when she saw the German planes flying over and would drop into terrible depressions. You see, she worried about everything and seemed to take the weight of the world upon her shoulders. The more worried she got the more she started to talk to herself, so I would keep out of her way. The cottage we lived in was a pretty little place with a cold water tap and electricity; quite modern for the time considering it was way out in the countryside. Of course it all changed in March of 1941."

My curiosity was spiked. I had to know more. "Why was March 1941 so important?"

"Well that was when Virginia killed herself," said Marie quite matter of factly. "I can remember it as if it was yesterday. We were all sitting around our little table having lunch when Leonard Woolf came hurtling in, red-faced and in a terrible panic. He was clutching some paper in his hand. He shouted, almost hysterically, that Virginia was going to kill herself. My Dad and

201

Leonard rushed out of the house and we all followed behind and started searching the river bank. My Dad found her walking stick on a muddy slope down to The River Ouse, but there was no sign of her. You see, she had planned it very well. She always knew that Leonard came in to listen to the war news on the radio at midday. She had placed the note by the radio for him to find, but left much earlier. She did not want to leave any chance of being saved."

"The poor woman was convinced that she was going mad; she was hearing voices again and decided she could go on no longer. She suffered terribly from her black depressions, it was so sad to see. Her last book was not selling well and it all mounted up until on that spring day in 1941, she could stand it no longer. She loved Leonard dearly and they were always so sweet together but no one could save her. They found her body a few weeks later nearly a mile away. She must have washed up and down the river with the tides. When they found her she still had stones in her dressing gown pockets, which she had collected along the river bank. Leonard had her cremated. He and my Dad scattered the ashes under her favourite Elm tree in her garden, where she used to sit in the summer and hum to the birds. Leonard stayed at Rodmell until he died many years later. His ashes were scattered under the same tree but that blew down in a great storm. I do believe there is a bust there to mark the spot now. Strange old life we lead, isn't it?"

"Oh Marie you're so right. There is an old saying up north, " 'now't as queer as folk'."

"Alex, you can say that again and the longer I live the stranger we all seem, but it has been lovely. I was thinking of having that on my gravestone, 'IT WAS LOVELY WHILE IT LASTED'."

I had to smile and thought how appropriate.

"Marie, your Bernina is singing like a new machine. I expect it will last many more years."

"See me out then," Marie laughed.

"Oh it will se us both out and a few more as well."

I left Marie's home, amazed by her story but not taken aback. Over the years I had heard so many amazing tales that little seemed to take me by surprise anymore. There seems to be a combination of circumstances that take place to bring around a good story. Firstly, my customer has to stay with me at the machine, they also have to be in the right mood as I am concentrating on the machine and not saying much, and most importantly they have to feel like talking. I had visited Marie many times but this was the first time in over 20 years that she had told me her fascinating tale.

From Marie's I cut down the lanes and narrow roads into Lewes, right by Harveys Brewery where the cold wind was busily spreading the malt and barley steam (coming from the main chimney) across the town, so that the workers rushing to their jobs could get a taste of their legendary elixir. From the town I headed north to Malling Down, then right at Earwig Corner and through the pretty village of Ringmer, pointing the old girl up The Broyle along the B2192 towards Halland where my next customer, a retired tailor, was waiting with a faulty switch that needed bypassing on his Pfaff sewing machine.

I passed Terrible Down Farm, then over a small stream to Terrible Down itself, just before the roundabout at Halland. You would hardly notice this place and a million cars buzz by it without a

204

Harveys Brewery is a Lewes institution. Founded in 1790 it has been filling the Lewes air with the smell of malt and barley ever since. Most Tuesdays the brewery sends out a special cart to deliver to the local pubs, much as they have done for over 200 years. My friend Dave, who is a drayman for Harveys, now drives a modern Mercedes lorry but still delivers the barrels of beer in a time honoured way.

clue as to its gory past. Terrible Down certainly earned its name, for legend tells that once the streams that feed the River Ouse ran red with blood from this place. There are several tales of how Terrible Down (or Turbyldoune as it used to be called) earned its name, but documents from recently discovered church records show that the real one was in May of 1264 when a long forgotten slaughter happened.

The Battle of Lewes had just taken place and Simon de Montfort and his troops were victorious against Henry III and his men. Henry had come to the throne as a boy of only nine when his father, Rotten King John, had died from dysentery in Newark Castle in the autumn of 1216. King John had spiralled downhill, even supposedly losing the Crown Jewels on the marshes. In truth, I would bet a week's wages that the jewels were probably shared out amongst the greedy barons in his entourage and they made up a story about losing them in the muddy Fens of Cambridgeshire. Some clever historian needs to dig up who was with King John when he died and see how they flourished after.

Anyway, Henry had followed in his father's footsteps constantly arguing with his barons and even the Magna Carta signed by his father at Runnymede had little power left in it. Once again abuse of 'royal clout' had led the powerful families of England to yet another battle, this time at Lewes. These old kings were warrior kings, they took to battle like kids to ice cream. The barons, many from the families who had come over with William in 1066, had grown fat on the land they had captured. As their own private armies had grown so had the resentment to their powerful overlord, King Henry. Henry on the other hand, would tax the landowners and then use it for war, often to fight his own unruly barons. The profits that kings made from successful campaigns in turn benefited churches, abbeys, cathedrals and universities. These established pillars of English society in turn paid grateful homage to their benefactors, even making the odd king a saint along the way.

Simon de Montfort had a much smaller army at Lewes and had sought peace terms but Henry was full of bluff and bluster. He had his son, Prince Edward, and his brother Richard, 'King of the Romans', with him. He also had Lewes Castle perched on top of the world. Basically there was no possibility of defeat and so he told Simon where to go. Battle was inevitable. Simon de Montfort, Earl of Leicester, and Gilbert de Clare, Earl of Gloucester, had gathered an army with many Londoners coming down from the capital to help fight the unjust King.

The big difference between the two armies was that the Barons Army was fighting for passion and belief and the Kings for more money, land and power.

This was a pivotal battle in English history and much of the political system we have today stems from this turning point in

our past. The battle was ferocious with both sides gaining minor victories, but a fatal cavalry charge by Prince Edward (to attack and destroy the Londoners) took a vital part of Henry's army away from the main action. By the time Prince Edward returned with the news of his success in battle, Lewes was ablaze, with the King sheltering in Lewes Priory. His brother Richard was holed up in a windmill and both were surrounded by Simon de Montfort's barons. Defeat and surrender were the only possibilities left and when orders were given to unleash a volley of fire arrows to set the priory ablaze, the King finally surrendered. Terms were agreed with Henry's son to be held as hostage.

However, as the outcome of the battle became obvious, some of the king's men managed to retreat out of Lewes and made a mad dash for home, a group taking the old toll road to Halland. By late afternoon word had reached the victorious barons that a sizable amount of troops had gathered near Halland. To the barons this could be a group of worn-out troops, resting for the night, or it could be a force of the King's men uniting to make a rescue attempt!

Simon and his barons quickly agreed that if the King or his son started another war, any reasonably sized body of loyal men could cause big problems (how right they later turned out to be) so the order was given for the cavalry to destroy the remnants of the retreating army.

They caught up with the King's men just before nightfall not a mile out of Halland on a slight rise (called a down by our Saxon forbears). Exhausted and in disarray, the retreating infantry had dumped most of their armour and weapons in Lewes earlier, when they ran for their lives.

It must have been a bloodcurdling sound at the camp when they heard the heavy cavalry charging up the hill towards them. They were helpless against the mighty steel-protected chargers and bloodthirsty knights. As darkness fell a great slaughter took place and the name Terrible Down was forever born in blood.

It did Simon de Montfort little good. Just over a year later he was defeated and killed at the Battle of Evesham by the long legged Prince Edward (who had escaped from captivity and rounded up a new army just as the barons had feared). The Crusader King, Edward went on to become the infamous King Edward I, hammer of the Scots.

Simon's head was hacked off at Evesham then tarred and mounted on a pike. It was then marched, with great fanfare around the country to all the larger towns and cities as an example of what happens to traitors who take arms against their king. His head was a great spectacle, causing crowds to gather on market days and the local taverns had a boom selling extra pies and ale.

However, in all the carnage and brutality of medieval England something amazing was born that day. The Battle of Lewes is commonly believed to be a landmark in the political evolution of our country. At that point in history the first steps towards monarchs being properly accountable to their government started. When Henry was captured he agreed to The Mise of Lewes, basically agreeing to everything that the Barons asked.

The other option on the table for him was a quick death! The following year on 20th January 1265 the first English Parliament was held at Westminster.

The actual Mise of Lewes (whatever it was) did not last long. In fact, Henry and his son later managed to destroy all records of it so we don't know for certain what humiliating terms it contained. However it planted the political seeds which grew into the democratic society in which we live today. Awful for the poor soldiers running for their lives at Terrible Down that evening in May of 1264, but great for the rest of us today! Like most democracies the path to our freedom was a long and bloody one.

My customer in Halland had started his working life as a trainee apprentice at the famous Austin Reed bespoke suit makers. For

a hundred years Austin Reed have made suits for the rich and famous from Cary Grant to Richard Burton, Tommy Cooper to Winston Churchill, their quality and skill is world renowned. They have many outlets and a plush flagship store on Regent Street, London and employ over 1,000 people in over 120 shops. At the moment they are in big trouble as competition from cheaper imports and off-the-peg suits have left them on the verge of bankruptcy. Only time will tell if they can survive.

One of their main manufacturing units was in Kingston, Surrey. At Kingston they took school leavers and trained them in a special department before they would be paired up with one of the experts, be it pattern cutting, shirt making, or bespoke tailoring.

There was a great joke that the head teacher told in the apprentice room to break the ice and relax the new lads. This is how it was told to me and I am going to end this story on it. I thank Austin Reed for my best laugh of the day.

A middle-aged man goes to his doctor for he is having constant headaches and nothing seems to help. After prescribing several pills with no effect the doctor tells his patient that he needs to see a specialist; he has a colleague in Harley Street who could help. After tests the Harley Street Specialist breaks the bad new to the man that his testicles are pressing against the base of his spine causing nerve problems up his back – leading to his terrible headaches. His recommendation was to remove the testicles as now that he was middle-aged he didn't really need them. The patient thought long and hard and decided that he would prefer to be headache free and reluctantly booked the operation.

211

Some months later the man walked out of hospital pain free. For the first time in over 20 years he had no headache. He was euphoric knowing that he had made the right decision. Feeling on top of the world, as he passed Austin Reed's in Regent Street, he made the impulsive decision to buy his first new suit for two decades.

In the measuring room was a short bald man with half-rimmed spectacles perched on his nose and a tape measure round his neck. He dutifully took all the man's measurements, saying them out loud to his assistant who jotted them down. When the tailor got to the customers waist and inside leg he called out, "34 long crotch." The customer politely interrupted and explained that he is actually a 34 short and has proudly been wearing the same size of trousers for 20 years! "Oh no, no, sir," replies the tailor with a very worried expression, "If you have a 34 short crotch, you would crush your testicles against your spine and get the most awful headaches!"

WALTER HUNT
THE FORGOTTEN GENIUS

"All in all Walter Hunt
has probably tried for more inventions
than any American alive to date."
New York Tribune 1857

Walter Hunt 1796-1859

Many readers will know that I undertake a lot of research for my website, Sewalot.com. The site is all about 19th Century sewing machines and their pioneering inventors. It is currently the number one site of its kind in the world. However, in my books I hardly write about the 'sewing machine kings' that make my trade possible so I thought I would put it right here and write briefly about one of the most interesting characters of them all.

Out of the sewing machine pioneers that I have dug up, Walter Hunt stands head and shoulders above the rest. Hardly anyone knows his name today but in reality he should be up there with the other pioneers such as Elias Howe and Isaac Singer.

Walter Hunt was one of the most prolific inventors in American history and in reality probably invented the first lock stitch sewing machine in the world. Many of his inventions are still in use today; the safety pin, the sewing machine, the fountain pen, Walter invented everything from ice breakers for ships to repeating rifles, nail making machines to safety lamps. My

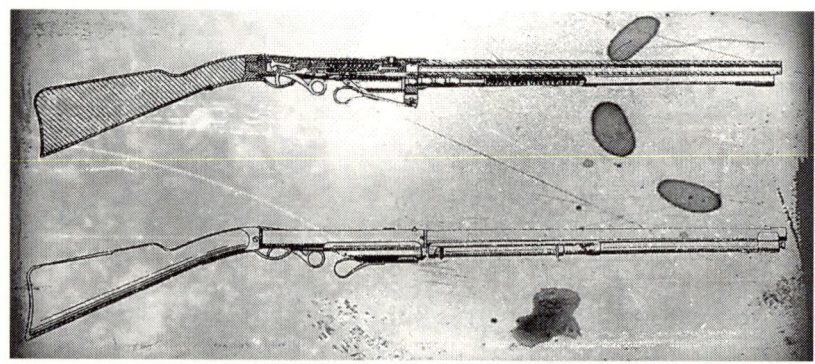

Walter Hunt's repeating rifle was extremely accurate due to the long rifled barrel.

personal favourite is a simple but brilliant invention; a reversible metal heel for shoes.

So why doesn't every school kid know his name? We know Edison and Bell, Faraday and Voltaire, but Hunt! Who was he? And more importantly why is he so ignored?

Walter Hunt died of pneumonia in June of 1859 aged 63 after falling ill in his workshop, still inventing. He left behind an almost silent legacy of genius. Why was it silent? Because our American inventor had a fatal flaw. He was an inventor, not a businessman, something that his son George W. Hunt was to rectify when selling his ideas, but that was too late to make his father rich and famous.

Walter was one of the first pioneers of the sewing machine and ended up fighting nearly every patent holder and manufacturer of sewing machines in his volatile court life. In the end he gained nothing.

Walter spent nearly 15 years fighting court battles to prove and secure some of his amazing inventions. Some were financed by

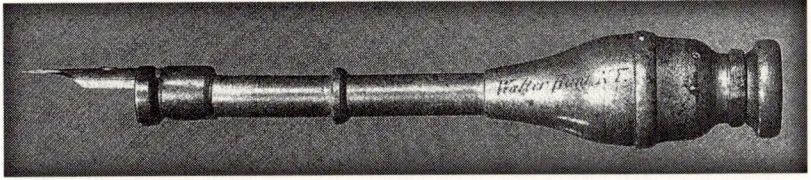

Walter Hunt's refillable fountain pen of 1847 was years ahead of its time. He went on to patent several ink filling pots. I love the plunger, it is like an early syringe. Why did he not make the profits Parker Pen did? It was, and still is, all about rights and marketing.

Isaac Singer who paid for Hunt's action against Elias Howe. Unfortunately Walter was born, like most of us, without wealth. He had to struggle to make ends meet and pay the rent. Had he been born wealthy he may have been one of the most famous inventors ever!

His humble beginnings in Martinsburg, New York meant that every time he had a stroke of inventing genius he sold it to pay off debts or simply to buy food and keep a roof over his family's head. This was a pattern that he repeated over and over with his inventions. He would spend all his efforts on inventing a new product, often not even paying to patent it, then sell it to the highest bidder.

No one knows how many things Walter actually invented but we do know it is many more than we have records of. He was well known for selling ideas quickly so he could start his next project.

Let me explain why I call him an inventive genius. Let's look at his safety pin. Anyone could make it so where is the genius? The genius is inventing something that had never existed before. Take the Phillips head, all screws had flat grooves in them until Henry Phillips came up with the simple but brilliant idea of his cross-head screws.

Walter's lack of long-term vision in business would leave him respected in his local community but a virtual unknown to history. When Walter invented his sewing machine in the 1830's there were no patents on them, no machines that sewed properly with a lock stitch even existed. Within two decades there were thousands of patents covering all aspects of the sewing machine.

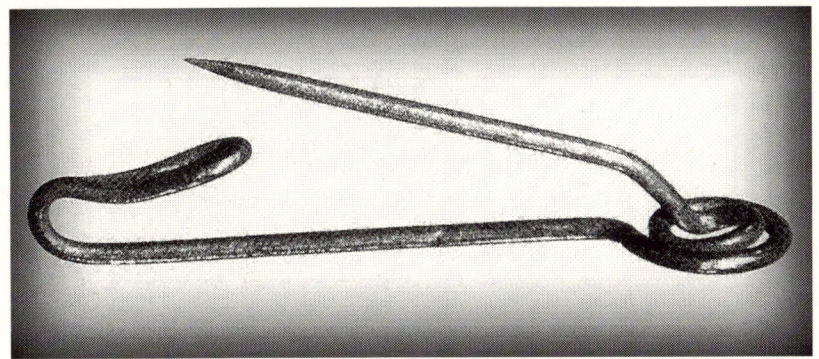

Walter Hunt's Safety Pin of 1849. The double twisted lower part was unique. He would have made millions from this one invention had he kept some of the rights and a profit share. Once someone had seen how the safety pin worked they could easily copy and improve on it.

Other pioneers in the sewing machine field who managed their patents with vigour and aggression, like Elias Howe and Isaac Singer became the wealthiest men of their generation with their names forever cast in stone.

So where did Walter's amazing journey begin? He was the eldest of 13 children, born on July 29th 1796 into a farming community in Martinsburg, New York. His mother, Rachel, had her hands full bringing up a whole coach load of kids. His father, Sherman, would have found his children useful as they grew, working on the farm or bringing in money from local jobs.

Fancy having 13 kids! In no particular order they are, Walter, Almira, Hiram, Harry, Philo, Albinos, and Adoniram (who became a crucial part in his later sewing machine invention). Then there was Levisa, Enos and Sherman. Angelina, Elizabeth and Hanna. Give me strength, I'm worn out just thinking about them, imagine the washing!

As a child Walter spun wool and cotton alongside his brothers. This was to prove a useful grounding for his later invention of the sewing machine. At the Lowville Textile Mill in Lewis County, Walter's genius started to show. He invented several flax, wool and cotton spinners to help production at the mill and was soon in demand being head-hunted by the owners at Willis Hoskins Mill (also in Lewis County).

However Walter, now a young married man with a wife and children wanted more and found his future calling to him from New York City.

New York in the 1820's was buzzing and Walter was constantly attracted to the excitement of city life. It was also in the big cities where people could find work and young inventors could find buyers for their ideas. In 1827 Walter, now over 30, decided to move his family to the city where he would make and sell his inventions.

Walter started to look at land to make money rather than inventions and for a while he was a successful real estate dealer. In 1828 Walter was doing very nicely with land speculation along the Hudson River area. New streets were being opened up and leases were for sale. Walter made thousands in land leases, which goes against current Internet records telling people he was just a poor old inventor. While he made a good living in land development Walter was still inventing and in 1829 he patented his spiral twisting machine for hemp and cotton to quickly mass produce lengths of rope.

These inventions and land leases allowed Walter to live in his first substantial house in Amos Street. Here he built a small workshop and a studio for his paintings, in which he indulged during moments of leisure.

In 1831 Walter helped Levi Kidder, his friend and neighbour, to patent a water cistern. His mind was always like a whirlwind and any tiny trigger would move him in an inventive direction. For example, on a trip to New York Walter had witnessed a needless accident when a child was injured by one of the thousands of horse-drawn carriages that crammed the streets. A simple alarm could possibly save lives and Walter soon invented a foot-operated bell (forerunner to the car horn) to warn pedestrians and other coaches. As usual he simply sold his idea and forgot about it.

Later in his life this 'invent-and-sell' attitude was to have serious consequences for his wealth. His mind was always alive with ideas. His safety pin was invented while talking to a friend. Walter was simply bending a piece of wire that he had picked up from his workshop floor. He realised he could form a new pin that was unique and could be patented.

In 1833 Walter and his family moved to 22 Asylum Street, New York. Walter was always impatient and was soon moving again to Bedford Street. As he became a respectable business man in his community he was worth reporting on, and the papers noted that 'the Hunts seem to move with the seasons'.

Once settled, Walter worked seriously for many months building his sewing machine, a unique invention in the history of the world, using a curved needle with the eye at the bottom and a small metal shuttle. By 1834 he had built his machine partially out of wood and played with it to perfect the formation of the lock stitch. This is where his early training in the cotton mills paid off as the use of the large wooden shuttles in the looms were his inspiration for his small metal shuttle on the sewing machine.

THE LEGEND OF FRANCES HUNT

There is an old tale amongst sewing machine collectors and enthusiasts that it was Frances Hunt who made her father give up the idea of patenting his sewing machine. Frances always took a great interest in her father's inventions and when he started building his sewing engine Frances became deeply worried about the plight of the workers who were sewing by hand. If a machine could be made that did the work of ten women then it seemed obvious that nine of the women would soon be out of work!

The tale goes that a huge argument erupted one evening between Frances and her father. It makes sense that Frances was right, women were already amongst the lowest paid workers and they were having enough trouble making ends meet as it was. Throw in a new-fangled machine that did their work many times faster and the writing was on the wall that many people would suffer.

In America alone, tens of thousands of women were employed in the manufacture of goods sewn by hand. Frances and Walter continued their heated discussions about what would happen when his machine came onto the market and Walter was eventually convinced by his daughter to give up on patenting his invention.

Of course history shows us that Frances was completely wrong and the exact opposite happened to what she had worried about. Far from take jobs away from women the sewing machine created millions of extra jobs all around the world as mass production blossomed.

Back in 1834 no one could have foreseen the amazing boom to industry the sewing machine made and the countless jobs it would create. Several people, including Mahatma Gandhi, said it turned out to be one of the most useful inventions in history.

Eventually Walter sold his machine without perfecting it to Geo Arrowsmith, and as many times before Walter moved on. Only when his brother, Adoniram (paid by Geo), copied Walter's machine in metal and made improvements, did it actually sew a reasonable stitch. It had no patent protection, something that was later going to cost Walter a fortune and make his future enemy, Elias Howe rich, but we will come to that shortly.

Walter's sewing machine was not practical but it was a sewing machine, even using two reels of sewing thread. Our inventor had sold his idea with little more than a simple handshake, no legal documents or proof for future law suits. When his brother perfected the machine in 1835 it was placed on display as 'a modern miracle' at the Globe Stove Company in New York.

Geo Arrowsmith had planned to raise money for mass manufacture and patents but this never happened and for a multitude of reasons the idea simply faded away. Years went by and the machine, which had been seen publicly and advertised extensively, disappeared never to be seen again.

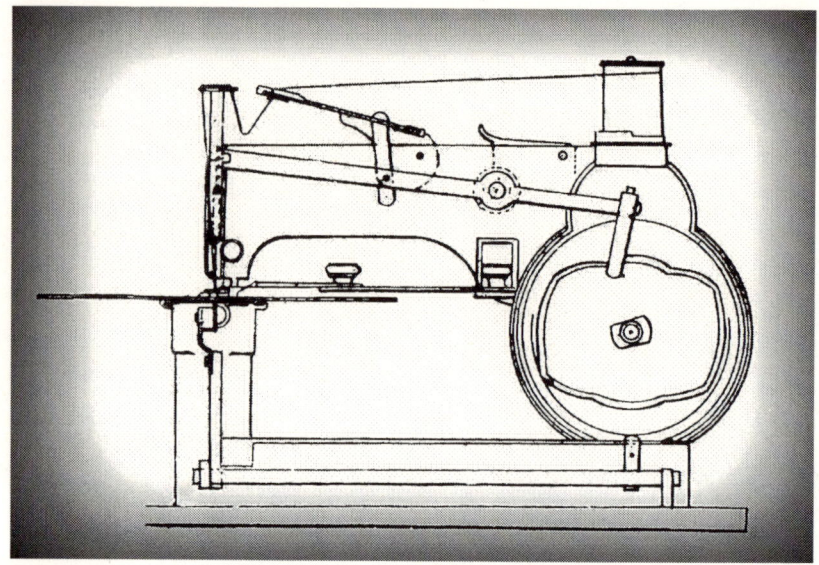

Walter Hunt's amazing lock stitch sewing machine was years ahead of its time. However there was one big fly in the ointment. Walter supposedly lost all his original plans and machine. This is a later plan, after he had seen many other sewing machines, and was locked in a patent battle with the formidable Elias Howe.

And so the first American lock stitch machine made by Walter fell from grace, until that is, money was being made in vast amounts from sewing machines by a handful of men who became known as The Sewing Machine Kings.

So now we jump ahead from the 1830's to the 1840's, and The Great Sewing Machine Wars.

In 1842 J. J. Greenough filed the first ever American sewing machine patent and in May of 1846 (the most important date in sewing history), Elias Howe Jr was awarded his patent for a lock stitch machine using two threads, a small metal shuttle and a curved needle with a point at the bottom end. Sound familiar?

Elias Howe held several important patents which crippled any mass production of sewing machines.

Both these main patents held by Howe were to cause The Sewing Machine Kings serious heartburn and no proper sewing machine could be made without using Howe's patents and consequently paying him royalties. Years had passed since Walter had invented his little sewing machine and argued with his daughter.

In the 1850's master litigator Elias Howe, had been successfully suing any manufacturer who dare make a sewing machine without paying him a licence fee, but he was attacked by Isaac Singer in an effort to break his stranglehold on the sewing machine patents. This in turn triggered The Great Sewing Machine Wars, creating the largest and longest court cases in American legal history.

However before we start The Sewing Machine Wars we have one more question to ask. Did Elias Howe ever see Hunt's sewing machine all those years before at the Globe Stove Company, while it was on public display? It is a question that we shall never know the answer to. All the court cases that were to follow over the next few years show a clutch of very dubious characters, all swearing under oath different versions of their own truths.

It had all kicked off when Elias Howe arrived back in America in April of 1849 after trying to sell his overpriced sewing machine all over Europe. One corset manufacturer in London bought the rights to it but that was about all. However when he arrived home he found that the Industrial Revolution had been moving fast in his absence and several companies were making sewing machines. These machines were using ideas that were similar to his and covered by his patents. Elias went to war. His costly patents were being infringed by every Tom, Dick, and Harry! Howe double-mortgaged his father's farm and went on to sue just about everyone he could.

Elias Howe's early litigation success gained him wonderful wealth. With his money he became more ruthless. But..., oh yes there is a but! In marches the flamboyant Isaac Merritt Singer; six foot five inches of showman, actor, inventor and cold-blooded businessman.

Isaac Singer was the most flamboyant man in the sewing machine business and a glorious character. When the average height at the time was little over five feet, Isaac in socks, stood around six foot five and had a shock of wild hair. In shoes and top hat he was an imposing seven foot powerhouse of a man who women found irresistible. As a young man he was a womanising devil. As an old man, with around 24 children, he was married to a half French model 30 years his junior.

The two men hated each other with a passion, coming to blows more than once. In 1853 Isaac Singer was in a protracted court case with Elias Howe (who seemed to be suing him on a daily basis and providing the periodicals with wonderful entertainment) when Isaac came up with a cunning plan to break Elias's domination of the sewing machine industry. Isaac had heard rumours of Hunt's machine and he tracked down Walter Hunt and paid him a nice lump of money to resurrect his old sewing machine. Unfortunately, Walter's old part wooden machine, and his brother's metal machine had both long gone and as much as huge searches were made, neither were ever located.

Isaac's idea was simple, to try and gain a patent backdated for Walter's 1834 machine or at least prove Howe was not the inventor and make his patent useless. Even if he did not overturn Howe's patents, Isaac could destroy Howe's public persona and thus damage Howe's business that way.

Unfortunately no one could produce the old machines and even more suspiciously all the plans were also lost!

Of course in 1853, almost 20 years after Walter had made his machine, the idea of obtaining a patent was ridiculous. Mind you the lawyers were not going to tell him that. They were making a mint in court. Walter applied for a patent for his sewing machine invention, but in the spring of the following year it was refused on the ground of abandonment. Incidentally when Isaac Singer had seen the writing on the wall he had secretly made an agreement with Elias Howe and others to form an illegal combination.

This is hard reading but utterly fascinating… Judge Charles Mason, Commissioner of Patents, May, 1854

"Hunt claims priority upon the ground that he invented the Sewing Machine previous to the invention of Howe. He proves that in 1834 or 1835 he contrived a machine by which he actually effected his purpose of sewing cloth with considerable success. Upon a careful consideration of the testimony, I am disposed to think that he had then carried his invention to the point of patentability. I understand from the evidence that Hunt actually made a working machine in 1834 or 1835. The papers in this case show that Howe obtained a patent for substantially this same invention in 1846.

Notwithstanding this, the Commissioner was forced to refuse Hunt's belated application, for the reason that an Act of Congress in 1839 had provided that inventors could not pursue their claims to priority in patents unless application was made within two years from the date when the first sale of the invention was made. Hunt had sold a machine in 1834, and had neglected to make application for his patent till 1853.

Thus it was that one of the grandest opportunities of the century was missed by the man who should rightfully have enjoyed it; the honors and emoluments of the great sewing machine invention passed to a man who neither had invented a single principle of action, nor applied a practical improvement to principles already recognised

Judge Charles Mason then went on to attack Elias Howe who had invented his own sewing machine and patented in in 1846…

Elias Howe, Jr., acquired the power, by simply patenting another man's invention, to obstruct every subsequent inventor, and finally to dictate the terms which gave rise to the great Sewing Machine Combination about which the world has heard – and scolded – so much. Howe's machine was not, even in 1851, of practical utility. From 1846 to 1851 he had the field to himself, but the invention lay dormant in his hands. He held control of the cardinal principles upon which the coming machines must needs be built, and planted himself squarely across the path of improvement – an obstructionist, not an inventor – and when, in 1851, Isaac M. Singer perfected the improvements necessary to make Hunt's principles of real utility to the world Howe continued to obstruct and pursue litigation."

Walter Hunt testified, under oath, as follows…

"Elias Howe has several times stated to me that he was satisfied that I was the first inventor of the machine for sewing a seam by means of the eye-pointed needle, the shuttle and two threads, but said that it was irrelevant as he had the prior right to the invention because of my delay in applying for letters patent."

The final court ruling was that Walter Hunt had in fact invented the first practical sewing machine but would not be given a patent as it had been on public display and hence any patent protection was automatically void.

Elias Howe Jr had won against Walter Hunt and Isaac Singer. From that point on Elias Howe got seriously wealthy but did not live long enough to enjoy it, dying at the tender age of 48.

In 1854 Walter Hunt did patent parts of an improved sewing machine that had not been covered by Howe in his original design but it was all too late, the horse had long since bolted.

Isaac Singer had been outmanoeuvred by the ever stubborn Elias, and was left bitter, twisted and in debt. He tried to get out of paying Walter Hunt for his time and effort. Another row ensued with Singer, as usual, all bluff and bluster. At the time he was living with at least three women in New York (at the same time) so he was used to lying through his teeth!

To make things even worse for Walter Hunt, Isaac Singer had secretly joined forces with the man he hated, Elias Howe (and a few others) to create the artificial monopoly called The Sewing Machine Combination. Basically their hate for each other was tempered by the wealth they were going to gain when all the main sewing machine patent holders combined and sued every new factory in America that was making sewing machines, the 'must have' gadget of the day.

Suddenly Singer had no more use for Walter Hunt and unceremoniously dismissed him with no further payments. Walter protested but there was little he could do against the mighty Singer who was rapidly rebuilding his fortune.

Years later, after many of the sewing machine pioneers were dead, including Singer, Hunt and Howe, the courts finally found in favour of Walter Hunt about the payments that Isaac Singer should have made to him during the Howe fiasco. The courts made the huge Singer Corporation cough up for Isaac's old promises. The money went to Walter Hunt's, widow, Polly and their children. But let's get back to the final part of Walter's story.

After losing in court against Howe, Walter did not sit on his laurels for long and he soon got onto more inventions such as automatic collar folding machine for shirts and suits. Walter carried on inventing right up to his sudden death in 1859.

I get the feeling that Walter Hunt was a nice bloke, perhaps too soft when facing giants like Elias Howe and Isaac Singer. Something I never felt from Singer or Howe while researching them. Perhaps a man of honour and character.

There is a final twist in our tale. When Walter died, a well-off but not overly rich man, he was buried in Green Wood Cemetery, Brooklyn, New York. In 1870, Polly, his long suffering wife passed and was buried next him. They have a nice memorial, a small pinnacle of granite. In 1890 Elias Howe's remains were dug up and moved to the same cemetery. His monument is huge and opulent. The wealth he had gained in life soon vanished but not before his final legacy! His large cenotaph now casts a shadow over the very man who may have actually invented the first American shuttle sewing machine. How ironic.

And so we come to the end of one of the most fascinating inventors in history that most people have never heard of. It reminds me of something my mum always said...
"Always remember the golden rule. The one with the gold, makes the rule!"

THE GREAT BRITISH SEWING BEE

Over the years I have often been asked to do a bit of television work, mainly because of my website Sewalot.com which is all about the pioneers of 19th Century sewing machines. They would ask me to act as the 'specialist' consultant or provide in-depth knowledge of a particular sewing machine and its inventor or sometimes just their values. However, though I was always happy to supply any information, I always resolutely refused to be filmed. I never minded giving advice, like on one of the latest Sherlock Holmes movies. There was a scene (that was cut) of Jude Law and Robert Downey Jr rushing through a Jewish workshop in 1890's London, which was full of machinists making clothes. Though it turned out to be irrelevant, I supplied all the information for that scene and many more. I am often the silent help behind the scenes, providing details and values to auction programs and films. But, I have never once stood in front of the camera. That was until I was caught by The Great British Sewing Bee!

Love Productions, the team behind the series, brought positive persuasion to a whole different level. They are responsible for a mass of television programmes for all the major channels, everything from Benefits Britain to The Great British Bake Off with Paul Hollywood. The Great British Sewing Bee was becoming one of the BBC's most popular series and these babies were not going take no for an answer.

It had all started innocently enough, a little bit of information here and there for what they called their VT clips, the extra segments that they fill the programmes up with. They explained that although they were in the television industry and onto a good thing they knew nothing about sewing machines or the sewing industry. At first it was the odd telephone call or e-mail as I laid out countless suggestions on what clips they could film. But as the series got into full swing, with great viewing figures, the pressure grew. Suddenly I was taking conference calls where I was talking to a whole room full of 'London Luvvies', "We need to think outside the box Alex, you know brainstorm a little, throw a few ideas up and see how they stick." The problem was that they had no ideas, so these sessions should have been called 'let's suck Alex's brain dry'.

At the end of the sessions I would feel ravaged. Then e-mails would blast through from many of the different 'project managers' or 'freelance editors' coming up with all the ideas that I had just suggested, as if it was their brainwave. I was happy to go along, (as I had done many times in the past) but then came the clanger. "Alex we have seen some of your YouTube blogs and we believe you have 'television presence'. We were thinking of asking you to teach Claudia Winkleman how to sew. How do you feel about that?" I put them straight very quickly. "You have more chance of seeing me dance with a polar bear in a tutu than teach a TV celeb how to sew." They were a little let down but polite and always charming. The phone would go quiet for about a week and then a new charismatic voice would have a go in a different direction, "We were wondering if you could come up to London and introduce one of our VT clips. No…, well perhaps on a subject to your liking?" Each time they approached me in the sweetest manner looking for my weak spot, where I might just crack and crumble, but each time I held firm.

The pestering continued on several fronts from what seemed to be a dedicated 'harass Alex team' but I stood my ground –, advice yes, filming no. After a few months I was cracking. I think I just needed some peace. Eventually I told a lovely girl called Nelda that I might be persuaded to do a talk on a subject close to my heart and that very few people knew about. When sewing machines were first invented they were so expensive that few ordinary folk could afford them. Edward Clark, Isaac Singer's business partner, came up with a stunning scheme he called 'hire purchase.' It was a big risk as it basically meant giving someone that you did not know your product and trusting them, over a number of years to pay for it. Today it is commonplace but in the 1850's it was a brand new idea. This wasn't the local loan shark or moneylender but a fully regulated part payment scheme for ordinary everyday people. The results were amazing and in the first year alone sales of sewing machines went through the roof. Hire purchase was here to stay and now covers almost all the expensive items that we buy.

And so I had finally crumbled and agreed, but there were still sticking points. I refused to go up to the studios and film with the celebs. After another week it was them who cracked and offered some neutral ground, a sewing machine museum in Balham High Road, Wimbledon. I said no again. Eventually they surrendered and said that they would bring the entire film and sound crew down to my house and somehow cut it into the programme to look like I was up where it was all happening. "Now you've done it Alex," said Yana after I had hung up. "I heard you say you would do it and there's no going back with a team like that."

"It might not be too bad. Hey I might even enjoy it!"

"Oh, that's if you don't die while they are filming you."

"Damn, never thought of that one. Still, I have agreed now and when it is done they have promised to leave me alone. Apparently they only need about 90 seconds of film for the clip." Ninety seconds, more fool me.

In the run-up to filming I perfected my research and honed it down to the agreed time. What I had no idea about was that for every minute that we see on television, several hours goes into making it. Boy was I in for a hiding.

Before all that happened I needed to preen myself. I knew how awful some of these live programmes can look when they grabbed a stranger off the street, warts and all. I also knew that there would be no make-up ladies so I moved my brightest light to a mirror and examined the reflection. I was trying to see what Nelda had meant by 'television presence'. If they meant a fat spotty man with hair protruding from most orifices then I was the business.

I made a list of essentials to make me presentable. Firstly get a smart haircut, then buy some good tweezers and start pulling hairs. Sometime later, with a torch in one hand and my new Boots tweezers in the other, I went into plucking mode. I plucked until my eyes streamed, my ears burned and my nose was on fire. Next the eyebrows. My big bushy eyebrows needed taming. I rested for a day to allow my face to recover and then went to work on the forest over my eyes. For days I went out to my customers to fix their machines then came home and started to manicure. It made me realise and appreciate what women have to go through. The week before filming I made sure I wore gloves and cleaned under each nail and used moisturiser until my workman's hands looked almost respectable. By the weekend I was preened to perfection, every ounce the superstar.

I constantly practiced my words and basically worried myself sick. Then to my utter horror I awoke to find a huge spot had decided to appear on my nose. When I say huge, the pulsating red blob, like a cyborg's eye, was big enough to cast its own shadow! I lanced it with my finest needle and squeezed out the puss, carefully cleaning the area so that I did not get a rash of other spots. Then the IBS hit. My belly started gurgling, bubbling and basically just swelling up. I looked like a pregnant walrus. There was nothing to be done as the filming was planned for the following day.

I summed up my options – run for the hills, hike to Africa and try to find Livingstone, jump off Beachy Head, or in my condition, roll off it. In the end I decided to take my punishment like a man.

On the day of the filming Yana carefully put a dab of makeup on my spot and I paced around the house staring out of the windows.

Around midday I saw the first vehicles arrive; they circled like Indians. I had a sudden urge to whip out the back, leap the fence and make a dash for the alleyway but my shaky legs weren't taking me anywhere. I opened the door and in they came. Nelda smacked two big kisses on my red cheeks: "You're in show business now darling," she said as she breezed in. She was closely followed by the sound man from The Archers with boxes of gear and a cameraman from The Great British Bake Off. The men were followed by a drop dead gorgeous blonde in a smart pair of black trousers, loose fitting top and a silk scarf draped around an impossibly perfect neck. In her hand was a clipboard and some paperwork. "I'm Natalie," she whispered, shaking my hand. "We have spoken on the phone and I've been so looking forward to meeting you." I'm not sure if I replied or just dribbled.

While the sound and camera men started setting up in my spare bedroom, which I had carefully re-arranged with a collection of sewing machines, including a special one which was to be used for the demonstration. Nelda, Natalie, Yana and I started to get down to business refining exactly what I was to say and how to say it. I had already sent them the script so there were only a few minor changes and suggestions, always put forward in the most positive way. Looking back on it now they were probably just calming me down before the filming. Nelda went upstairs to see how the crew were progressing and left me with Natalie and the paperwork. "It's just a formality really, nothing to worry about" said Natalie as she handed me pages of documents. It was obviously her job to get me to sign a contract that no one had bothered mentioning. They had picked the perfect girl to do it, totally disarming in every way. Luckily I was only signing a contract for filming as I had little doubt that I would have signed just about anything she put in front of me.

I skipped through the pages trying to concentrate on the wording: 'worldwide rights', 'in perpetuity', words jumped out and danced around but I wasn't soaking anything in. It was all timed to perfection so that I could not get out of it. On the last page there was the remuneration, my pay, something that I had not even considered. All the research I had done, the endless discussions, calls and e-mails, the filming that I was to do and all the rights for the rest of time, was worth the wonderful amount of, wait for it…, one pound! "Oh it's just a token payment really," Natalie

My spare bedroom became a museum of bygone sewing machines as we all crammed in there for filming. Five hours later our 'ninety seconds' of filming was complete and ready for editing.

giggled, tossing her head back in an impossibly mesmerising way. "It just makes it all legally binding."

"Forever and a day I see." I laughed back. It had never crossed my mind to ask for remuneration so the pound was a bonus to me. "I think I will frame the pound and put it on the wall to remind me not to get caught again." Natalie smiled and I found myself signing my life away.

The spare bedroom had become a lightbox with assorted cameras, reflectors and lights transforming the room into a theatre. Nelda was perched on a stool opposite me as I was wired for sound. All around me the rest of the crew got to work to create movie magic! The funny thing with filming is that the viewer sees only what they want you to see. So there I was, seemingly all alone in my room talking to the invisible audience at home as they crammed in behind the camera. I chatted all about hire purchase and one of Singer's greatest sewing machines, the model 201k, made up in Kilbowie, Clydebank, Scotland. Hour after hour passed under the hot lights as I worked through the script to get those precious ninety seconds of film.

We stopped for a short break about three in the afternoon. Yana had knocked up one of her famous Victoria sponges. It was agreed by all that it tasted as good as anything they had eaten on The Great British Bake Off so Yana was a happy bunny. Filming resumed and by six o'clock we had it all sorted. "That's a wrap." Nelda announced, clearing up her notes.

With smiles, hugs and kisses, as if we were all best friends forever, they gathered up their paraphernalia and hit the road back to the big city and the editing desk. Nelda left us with strict instruction not to tell anyone about the filming. In my mind I knew the only way they would stop Yana from telling absolutely everyone was if a sniper took her out as they left. "Series Two, episode six," she added as she disappeared "You'll be famous."

As the last car vanished up Church Street I looked across at Yana and we both breathed out a huge sigh of relief. I said to her, "You know they never did give me that pound!" We both burst out laughing and went out for a meal to celebrate our freedom. Over the next few days my belly went back to normal and I calmed down. Even the spot on my nose disappeared. By the following week all the phone calls and e-mails had stopped, all the polite pestering gone. My perfect little world returned. Yana, like a

This is a shot from the television of how I appeared on the BBC in full flow after Claudia Winkleman's introduction. No one would have any idea of how cramped we were and how long and hot the filming was. It turned out to be a great success and now I apparently have a place called Sussex Sewing Museum...

skylark in spring, was unable to keep quiet and told just about everyone she met about the filming.

As the show aired I saw at first hand the miracle of television. How each scene, from Claudia Winkleman's seamless introduction at The Great British Sewing Bee warehouse in London, to my few seconds of fame fitted seamlessly into one Segway or VT clip. No one would ever have guessed all the work the crew had to go to and all the miles travelled for those few moments. The lighting and sound were perfect and you couldn't even see my missing tooth or notice the spot on my nose. No horrible hairs or dirty nails, it was all good and I was a happy boy. I couldn't help remembering Nelda's words: "You're in show business now darling." It really was movie magic. I also found a new respect for the endless hours of practice and effort that goes into making something on television look spontaneous and unrehearsed.

The next thing I knew Jane Hill from the Radio Times was contacting me asking for a feature. I gave her some basic information and once again politely declined. On the following day I went back to work a star. Now for those unlucky few of you that have never had your fifteen seconds of fame or bathed in the light of movie stardom let me tell you how it is.

The morning after the show aired, I was walking up a country lane to a small cottage near Gun Hill. It was a beautiful clear morning with a fresh breeze blowing through the valley, I had a spring in my step and my toolbox felt light in my hand. In the field a farmer was busily working away in his tractor. As I walked along I noticed that he was coming towards me. Then he made a couple of close passes staring straight at me. The tractor then drew level and shook to a halt. The door flung open and the farmer, a complete stranger, shouted, "Hey, ain't you that fella off the TV?" Embarrassed that on my very first call back to work I had already been spotted, I sheepishly grinned and shouted back, "Yes that's me."

"Well," he replied, "You're a lot fatter in real life!" Not waiting for an answer he slammed his door and I could see him laughing to himself as he rumbled up the field. Very funny, I thought as I carried on. The next day I was in a café in Bexhill enjoying a discreet coffee when Norman from Thimble-Inas, seeing an opportunity for a bit of fun, burst in. "You're that famous bloke," he shouted in the full café. In an instant the place, like a western saloon, fell silent and all eyes turned on me. "Can I have your autograph?" Norman shouted excitedly, like a teenager at a concert. "Here, sign my shirt. I love you." Next thing he was gone and I was looking for somewhere to hide. And so it went on until my fame, like the last frost of winter, disappeared as quickly as it had arrived.

After a few weeks I was once more invisible and allowed to carry on a normal life. However my friends, I must say that for a few moments I was up there flying with the gods. Quite honestly though, it is much better down here at ground level with all the normal human beings.

THE END

Herstmonceux Castle is a wonderful place and each year they hold a medieval fayre, which sets the castle and grounds off to perfection. If the castle was a woman it would be a superstar as it is almost impossible to get a bad picture of it.

Harvest time in East Sussex is something else; endless fields of ripe grain and haystacks in all directions. Even the earth smells glorious.

I drive by this old gate in Friars' Walk just off the High Street in Lewes several times a month and just love it. I have never found out where it leads or what is behind it but if ever there was a story waiting to be discovered it is there.

The Old Needlemakers in Lewes is now a host of specialist shops and cafés. Even on a rainy winter's day it looks stunning.

Apparently East Sussex has the largest amount of flint buildings in the world. This is the East Gate of Pevensey castle, an old Roman Shore Fort. It was later fortified by the Saxons, Normans and again in WW2. For around 2,000 years these old walls have stood proud. Some say a little drummer boy haunts the battlements and a grey lady walks the paths inside on certain spectral nights.

It is a fact that I do know just about every watering hole in my area and visit most of them on my rounds across the county. Here is Pooh Corner tea and gift shop in Hartfield. They have the sweetest mini tea garden where they do great cream teas.

Once again near Rickney on the back road to Herstmonceux. It was just before Christmas when I spotted some escaped turkeys. I assume they made a bolt for freedom when they saw some tinsel!

I came across these beauties by the side of the road near Hankham. They were basking in the summer sun and did not have a worry in the world.

I am constantly amazed at what I come across on my travels. Here are a pack of hounds being moved along a back lane near Rickney.

When you are out on the roads most days you can never tell why you are going to be late. This is the main Hastings road brought to a standstill by escaped cattle.

Raising money for charities is just a feel good thing to do and my wife Yana has perfected her 'Coffee Mornings' over the years. There is a huge amount of organisation that goes into each occasion and you can't imagine the work. However when it all ends well we can make another donation to help a local charity. Here is Yana making special bunting for her SeeAbility event.

It's all hands to the pumps when charity days come around.

Here is my wife Yana with our MP at the time, Stephen Lloyd, and Marlene, her mum. It really makes the charity day special when people make the effort to turn up and support it. Stephen Lloyd was always full of enthusiasm and support for anything in his constituency. Oh, and he loves a slice of cake.

It's no wonder I have a big belly. Someone has to finish off the cakes after everyone's gone.

The aftermath. Everyone has gone and the military operation to clear up begins. Most of the rooms look like a bomb has exploded and it can sometimes take a week to get everything in the house and garden back to normal.

This is The Elms in Rottingdean. The house was once the home of Rudyard Kipling but so many tourists came along the coast from Brighton to stare over the walls he moved to the isolated old manor at Batemans near Burwash.

Postcard pretty pubs seem to line every village street in East Sussex and none are prettier that The Tiger at East Dean. It is apparently where Sherlock Holmes retired to look after his bees. Well, that is what the plaque tells us on the wall near the pub!

I have had this old Daimler most of my adult life. When I bought her for £850 in the 1970's fuel rationing was on and they were mainly used for banger racing or just scrapped. Over the years we have been on many adventures across the Scottish Highlands and Europe. Now I seem to spend as much time under the car as driving it!

Having a classic car, I have chauffeured many of our friends to their weddings. If you are a chauffeur at such an occasion don't think it is just driving; you could be holding the brides dress out of the mud or, as here, acting as flower carrier.

The only time I was driven in my 1966 V8 Daimler was on my daughter Sarah's wedding day. It was a damp and cold spring day, yet full of happiness. I think I even fell asleep smiling.

Beachy Head is one of the spots that is used by pigeon racers to release their pigeons. Combines from up country like Yorkshire, and these from Greatham in Durham, travel through the night to get here. At the allotted time they release thousands of racing pigeons. For a few seconds the sky is full of noise and feathers as they figure out where they are and then they disappear homeward-bound into the distance in a great grey cloud.

This has to be one of the strangest things. At first sight a normal telephone box, but in fact it is Piddinghoe Village lending library. Just drop off and pick up books at your leisure.

This is the best place on planet Earth; my man cave. Originally a stable I have been tinkering with machines and all sorts in there for decades and have amassed just about every tool I will ever need. If I'm nowhere to be found then you can guess I am in the garage trying to fix something.

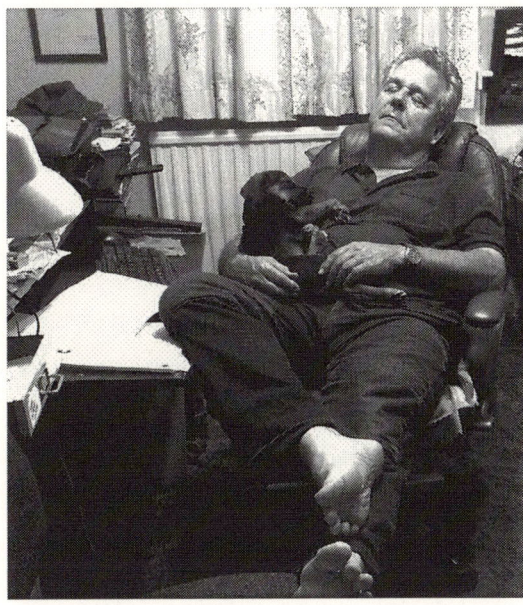

Feet up in front of the computer. When all the sewing machines are fixed and all the chores for the day done I can get down to writing. With Cilla to pester me sometimes I just give up and snore!

The Three Legged Pig

S pring had sprung early in East Sussex and suddenly our drab, grey world was blown apart. Whatever your beliefs spring is a miraculous time of the year. The barren black soil that seems to hold little promise of life suddenly bursts open, giving way to every shade of the rainbow, filling our winter weary eyes with colour. Within a short period our landscape transforms as trees bud and bushes blossom.

As I opened my front door I was greeted by snowdrops being teased by the tail-end of storm Imogen. The Fair Maids of February just make me smile; whatever the weather, warm or cold they seem to have a time clock that makes them appear in the second month of the year. While everything else was early they were, as usual, bang on time. I had to laugh to myself when I thought about the Met Office's brainwave last autumn to name the storms alphabetically. They probably thought that it would be years before they got to Z, but since Storm Abigail in November we were hit by one storm after another and now, just the second week in February of 2016 we were already on Storm

Imogen. The rate we were going they will probably have to come up with a new plan in no time at all.

A low sun was blinding me and with no clouds in the sky another little wonder was about to brighten up my garden, the fabulous lesser celandine. They are my all-time favourite early spring flower. Their bright yellow petals worship the sun like no other bloom and in early spring, with no chance of rain they would fully open their petals and follow the sun all day, closing to sleep just before sunset. The little beauties love our damp English soil and on bright days the petals not only open but curl to catch even more sun. Greek-ish for swallow, they often herald the start of spring and come out about the same time that our swallows arrive to prepare for a busy summer. Lesser celandine are a member of the buttercup family and it was also Wordsworth's favourite little gem. While we all remember that he wrote about his daffodils he also wrote at least three poems about the celandine. Many gardeners treat them like weeds, crazy or what? Even better than that they used to be called Pilewort as folklore told that they could cure piles. I have never found out how you were supposed to use them! I cherish each plant I have because my cheerful little Celandine make me happy.

I get a little poetical at this time of year; it's probably the sunshine after the dark hell of winter. It would not be long before the hawthorn blossom would turn the hedgerows white like fallen clouds, and when a cool breeze blows through them a trumpet blast of blossom will fall over the roads like confetti. The wood anemone and bluebells in the woods, that just moments before were so empty, will soon carpet the woodland floor in radiant whites and blues, and once again all will seem right with the

This is the old village pump on the Rushlake Green road above Foul Mile. The only time I ever notice it is in the spring when it looks so picture perfect.

world. All around, from the bleating balls of fluff to the birdsong, our lives will be filled with noise and excitement. With this rebirth, we come back to life as well. It charges our hearts and fills our souls, but most importantly it gives us hope, and that is a priceless joy.

I drove to my first call of the day at a farm down an old track in the middle of the Sussex wilderness. As I opened up the back of the car to get my toolbox out, a smiley dumpling of a woman puffed past, being tugged by an eager bundle of fur disguised as a golden retriever. "New pet" she wheezed, as she disappeared up a footpath into the woods. I didn't have time to reply but I thought that if I ever saw her again she would probably be half the size.

As I walked up the path an old farmer was leaning on a wall, enjoying the sun. He touched his cap and said in a drawl, "Morn." I could not help but notice that in his pigsty behind there was a plump pig nuzzling around in a pile of fresh feed, however it only had three legs! Unable to keep my curiosity from bursting out I had to ask the old farmer why his pig had a leg missing. "Well it's a strange old tale," he said. "That there is one special pig you're looking at. You put your toolbox down and I'll tell you a story." With my curiosity raised I did exactly what he said.

Now as it turned out, what he told me was actually his favourite three legged pig joke. When he finished I cried with laughter. What you have to imagine as you read on, is that old farmer with his yokel accent, straw in his mouth, pulling my leg something rotten.

"Well one day, before my first wife ran off with the apple picker and my kids were still at home," he said in his soft Sussex drawl, "I was working in the top field. Unknown to me the house caught fire and my son was in the house. No one heard a thing but that pig there did. He jumped over the sty, smashed straight through the front door and pulled my son out. Saved his life for sure."
"That's amazing," I said looking at the pig, "but why has he three

259

legs?"

"Oh that 'in't all. One day I was working in the bottom field and my daughter was in trouble in the lake. Well I never heard nothing what with the tractor makin' a din, but that pig did. He jumped over the sty, ran down the hill, leapt into the lake, and pulled my daughter to safety. Saved her life for sure."

"I'm astounded, that sure is a clever pig, but you still haven't told me why he only has three legs?"

"Ah well you see," said the farmer, chewing on the end of his straw. "One day my wife, the one that ran off with the apple picker, was trapped under a pile of hay bales that had fallen off a wagon. I didn''t 'ear 'er as I was in the middle field, but pig did. He leapt over the sty and dug my wife out and saved her life for sure."

"Well," I said in astonishment, "I have to admit that is one fantastic pig."

"Can't disagree there," says the old farmer nodding. "Maybe the greatest pig that has ever lived."

"But you still haven't told me why he only has three legs?"

"Ah," says the farmer, grinning a big old smile. "When you 'ave a pig as special as that, ONLY AN IDIOT WOULD EAT 'IM ALL AT ONCE!"

After howling with laughter I carried on up the path to the front door and as I rang the bell I looked back to see the farmer stroking his fat old pig. "Tell you his pig joke, did he?" asked his wife as she let me in. "It gets longer with each telling. He heard it somewhere and has added to it, dragging it on and on ever since. When he saw you drive up he knew he had a captive audience. "

"It is terribly funny," I replied and then asked her the real reason the pig only had three legs. Turns out that it was very old and had damaged his leg. A bad infection followed. Her husband loved it so much he paid a fortune to have the lower part amputated and the pig treated rather than lose his friend. I had to admit the pig seemed as happy as any pig I had ever seen.

By the time I left the pig was snoring in the sun. The farmer waved to me from his tractor, (possibly in his middle field). He was probably figuring out how to add a few more details to his pig joke 'Only an idiot would eat him all at once!' It still makes me laugh every time I think of it.

Jed the Farmhand
and his Broken Heart

His heart was broken, it was torn apart.
Now Jed's pain came from an innocent start.
As the country blossomed in an early spring,
He was filled with a burning from within,
For a local lass from the village pub,
Oh that Sally and her wonderful grub.

Pie 'n' chips, crusty ploughman's, shepherd's pie,
But 'twas not just the food that caught his eye,
For that buxom Sally had such a smile,
It could melt a man to a shaking pile.
He was besotted, all his reason gone,
Love being a funny thing, spurred him on.

So scrubbed and shinning in his only suit,
Fresh shaved, boots polished and looking real cute.
He headed for the pub on that fine day,
Bound for true love, to give his heart away.
A hand full of flowers picked from a field,
Walked into the pub and before her kneeled.

Suddenly silence, he felt his heart leap,
There it was hanging for Sally to keep,
His pure and untouched truly loving heart.
She laughed and grabbed it, then ripped it apart,
"You silly young boy" she playfully said,
"Why to love you I'd have to be brain dead."

The pub erupted in laughter and cheers,
Jed ran for his life, with eyes full of tears.
Dear Sally had shattered his fondest dreams,
For many days he planned sneaky schemes,
To get Sally back and the hurt she'd done.
But fate had not stopped, it was having fun.

It threw them together one stormy night,
And Sally found out that Jed was just right,
Now she is his wife, he loves her a lot,
So do the kids, even one in the cot,
Ah, but what of Jed's heart all ripped and raw,
Oh, that repaired one night in some dry straw!

A I A

HELLO HELLO!

I was standing on the doorstep of a beautiful old cottage on the borders of Westham and Pevensey. The glorious start to May had dragged people out of their hibernation and kick-started the yearly gardening frenzy. We wait patiently for spring, watching every movement in the ground and when it happens we are full of excitement, rushing outside and flinging our arms in the air praising creation. A few weeks later with the chiropractors and osteopaths doing a booming trade with bad backs and damaged limbs we're all thinking, "I wish the grass would slow down and give us a break." Before long I'm waking with night sweats thinking that the garden is creeping in the windows and pray for autumn.

Actually, for all my moans, I love gardening. It keeps me a little fitter and there is nothing more wonderful on earth than the smell in the evening air after a warm sunny day of spring growth. But then the army of bugs come marching in for a feast and another battle begins, arrgh! One of my regulars once said to me something profound wrapped up in the simplest of sentences; you never get angry gardening. How true it turned out to be.

At my customer's cottage, there were plenty of signs of life but no humans. I rang the front doorbell several times to no avail so walked around to the side of the house. The back door was open and the washing machine was rumbling away in the kitchen. I could hear the ball bearings had started to perish; those hard steel balls on which the world turns were giving up and everyone within a mile probably knew it. As the machine started its spin cycle a howl was emitted loud enough to bring back a few Roman soldiers to Pevensey Castle next door.

I had a problem – all the people had disappeared. With the door wide open I could see right through to the back door, which was also open – with the keys in it! The car keys were also on the table but no humans? I shouted, "HELLO?" No reply, so I shouted once more. Nothing! I walked around the side and shouted again. The garage door was ajar so I checked it out but there was no one in there. I then went back to my tool box, which I had placed inside the house and noticed that the alarm case was open and the alarm switched off. Well what to do? I searched the garden once more, nothing. I started to go inside and stopped. It was like an episode of Midsomer Murders and now I was suspecting that there were bodies piled up somewhere, behind the sofa perhaps?

I went in and stood in the kitchen scratching my head, trying to think of all the scenarios that could have taken place to make the family disappear from a million pound home, leaving everything behind. I shouted a few more times and then rang them from my mobile. That was stupid, I was standing right next to the phone I was ringing!

In my mind I summed up all my options. I was standing on the deck of the Marie Celeste. Trouble with me is that the first thought that came to my mind was to turn their coffee machine on. That wasn't helping!

I thought I might take one more stroll around their beautiful gardens as there was little chance of the homeowner shooting me. I mean the worst trouble in Westham was that the daily papers were sometimes late.

I stepped back out of the house and looked around. Pevensey and Westham are straight out of a picture postcard, two small villages, both with medieval churches joined by one road but split in two by the huge Roman/Norman castle. You could easily throw a stone from the castle walls into both High Streets. In times of siege the churches were used as battlements to shoot arrows into the castle and it suddenly hit me that I had stepped back in time. It was that quiet time of the morning with the kids at school and everyone at work, just before the oldies made their march on town. I felt like I had walked into the 1960's and any second I would see the milkman clattering up the drive. Postman Pat would wave to me from his red van with his evil little cat giving me the finger.

Then I heard the light tinkle of a woman's laugh in the distance. It was my first clue. There it was again. I walked up the garden path, passed the garage and through into another part of the garden, then round another corner and bingo, the husband, wife and gardener were all there chatting around his fork and sipping cups of tea. "There you all are. I thought you must have been kidnapped, but when I couldn't find a ransom note I started searching again." Three faces swung round to see me and then the woman laughed. "You know all your doors are open?" I added.

"Never mind, we only popped up the garden for a moment but got side-tracked. The worst thing that has happened here is when the old vicar, Gary Barratt, locked the bell ringers out of the tower a few years back and he's long gone now. Coffee Alex?"

"Yum, yes please" I said, walking back with her and leaving the husband and the gardener chatting about the size of the slugs this year. "I saw the sewing machine inside on the table" I added

267

picking up my heavy toolbox. I'll get stuck in."

Before long her machine was purring away and I was heading towards East Dean for my next call. I had a few customers in Westham and my favourite was Jane Bundy who lived in a superb ancient building on the High Street. It was so old that some of the rooms were below ground level where the road outside had built up over the centuries. She has gone to that great sewing room in the sky now and I miss her long chats about Westham life.

One of the most famous local characters that we often gossiped about was the amazing Margaret Spencer. When I say amazing just read on as she was unbelievable. If you saw her you would never know just how special she was. She had perfected her image as the little white haired old dear with huge glasses, who picked up her paper and occasional magazines at the local newsagents, or sat in at the local history group listening to others talk about the past. She loved helping out around Westham and engaged herself in many of the community projects, and everyone I met over the years had a kind word to say about her.

I often spotted Margaret walking along to St Mary's where she was the choirmaster. Margaret had a strange gait as she walked, which stood out. Whatever outfit or coat she was wearing I immediately knew it was her whenever I spotted her. Her amazing past came to life one day when I was standing on the doorstep of Jane's house at 41 The High Street and Margaret walked by to the church. "Morning," she said as she passed, "Lovely day." We both replied and she stopped for a chat. When Margaret went on her way we watched her awkwardly try and

Margaret Spencer in her youth.

speed up to get across the busy road. Jane leaned over and whispered, "Sniper bullet." I sort of shrugged and giggled a little as it caught me by surprise; Jane didn't normally joke like that. The she added, "She could snap your neck like a twig our Margaret." I was in a state of confusion trying to figure if Jane was kidding or not. She went on to explain about the best kept secret in Westham. Amazingly, the little old dear with the sweet smile and happy voice once led a double life. She was actually the secret agent codenamed Sister Evangeline.

Out of all the people that I have written about over the years Margaret Spencer may just be at the top of the list as the most astounding story of them all. There is definitely enough material for a Hollywood blockbuster. Maybe two!

Margaret never used to talk about her past as she had sworn an oath to uphold the Official Secrets Act. However, as she grew older and she outlived the protection time (which is 50 years) she shared a little insight into her secret life with her close friends in the village. In the late 1990's (when Margaret was in her eighties) more stories came out and eventually she became a local celebrity as her remarkable life unfolded. As her legend grew even the local paper ran a few of her stories. Margaret was a member of her local Women's Institute and gave a few talks about her life as a secret agent. That must have caused a few raised eyebrows at the meetings, although I have the feeling that she may just have taken the best stories with her to the grave.

When she was a young woman, at the beginning of World War Two, she enrolled into the Special Intelligence Services (which eventually mutated into MI6). As part of a small specialised team of six, Margaret, along with two other girls and three lads were intensively trained in all manner of undercover work including piloting, self-defence, unarmed and armed combat. After training, her daily apparel always concealed her service weapon, a Webley Colt 45, model 1911, semi-automatic British Service Model.

All the agents taught under the SIS had 'shoot to kill' training and Margaret had the bonus that her dad had taught her how to shoot (he was a crack shot and gunnery instructor).

Apparently the SIS was set up primarily to sabotage enemy operations and gather information. Its most famous department was Section D which organised home defence and conducted missions in Europe, I believe they later became part of Churchill's SOE, the Special Operations Executive. Eventually the SOE expanded to blowing up bridges and railways, trains and factories, and basically causing as much havoc as possible for the enemy.

It was dangerous work and the life expectancy of an undercover agent was close to zero! Two of the most famous agents who gave their lives were Jan Kubiš and Jozef Gabčík who died after they assassinated Hitler's 'Butcher of Prague', SS General Reinhard Heydrich. In May of 1942, as part of a small team, they carried out their suicide mission. They had parachuted into Czechoslovakia a few months before. They ambushed Heydrich (the main architect of the Holocaust) on his way to work from his castle a few miles outside Prague. The ambush went wrong when Gabčík's sten gun jammed but Kubiš tossed a grenade into the car wounding Heydrich (who later died of his wounds). Both the SOE operatives were hunted down and the German reprisals were horrendous with over 5,000 people murdered. I doubt if the mission would have gone ahead if the Allies had known what the Nazi's would do in retaliation. But war was war and in those desperate times Winston Churchill ordered all agents 'to set Europe ablaze'.

Margaret was taught to work alone in hostile territory. To begin with she used her training as a nurse as her cover. She moved around our coast to different hospitals, seeking out enemy infiltrators and spies, and then reporting her findings back to London via special operatives and contacts. During this period, secrecy was everything and not even her closest colleagues knew about her role as an agent. Even her husband Len just thought she was busy working long hours as a nurse! In fact many years later her daughter Diana said that because she was such a private person she only really wrote a fraction of what she accomplished down in letters to her family. She even turned down a publishing deal when it was offered.

Using her cover as a nurse and nun Margaret was sent on many undercover missions into Italy, France, and even Germany, being flown behind enemy lines at the dead of night. She used to laugh when she said that it must have been a very unusual sight to see a nun floating down from the heavens with her habit tucked into her knickers!

She took on the codename 'Sister Evangeline' when early on in the war she was exposed by a double agent in London, captured by the Gestapo and taken by the SS to one of their strongholds in France. Purely by luck, as she was being moved to head-quarters for interrogation, she passed two Frenchmen who spotted that she had her hands tied behind her back. Lucky for her they turned out to be in the French Resistance. They immediately realised what was happening and set a trap for the Germans. The car was blocked, the Germans shot and she was rescued and taken to a convent to recover. At the Convent of The Sisters of Mercy she noticed the clothes she had been given bore the name

Sister Evangeline. Her name codename was born.

After a period she was rescued and smuggled back to London. Her first mission was to track down the German double agent working at HQ. He was immediately arrested and 'dealt with'. Sister Evangeline went on to have more incredible life and death experiences throughout the war.

Just before the Normandy Landings in 1944 she was once more sent into action. Her orders were to gather information about the German troop movements. As D-Day took place she was dropped just outside Bayeux in Normandy. She was making her way towards Gold Beach and Arrowmanches when she came across a well defended part of the Atlantic Wall. The Resistance were supposed to have weakened the defences there to help the Allied troops through, but the defences were intact. The Resistance had all been captured and shot.

When Sister Evangeline realised what had happened she tried to get word back to London but D-Day was in full motion and so she decided to help out where she could. As the advance took place she spotted a trap that the Germans had set for the Allies in a village. She managed to shoot one of the German snipers who was in hiding, waiting for the approaching first wave to hit. After that she felt a thud in her back and a searing pain in the head. She later found out that she had been shot by another German who had spotted her. Then she was finished off with a rifle butt to the back of the head and left for dead. Luckily, after the village was freed someone in the advancing forces must have noticed that the dead nun on the floor was still breathing. The next thing Margaret remembered was waking up in a hospital in England,

She never found out who rescued her or how they got back to England, but she was always grateful to the unknown soldiers who saved her life.

While she was rehabilitating at Haslar Hospital she was told that the bullet embedded in her spine could not be removed. She would never walk again. However Margaret was made of sterner stuff and soon proved them wrong. It would take more than a bullet lodged in her spine to stop her.

During her recuperation she was moved to a hospital that had a separate building that specialised in caring for SIS operatives. Even there, in the spring of 1945, her training came into good use when she came across a stranger in the secure ward for agents, cross-examining a patient at gunpoint. Margaret immediately went into action. Always armed, she pulled out her Colt, burst in, and shot the gun out of his hand. He was captured and the patient saved. It was obvious that the hospital cover holding the special unit for agents to recover was blown so all the operatives were soon moved out.

Margaret's story gets even more astounding and I heard that she then moved to a protection team shadowing the two young princesses. This later led to the King personally thanking her. The Queen was so grateful when she met Margaret that she did the most unusual thing; she unpinned her favourite broach from her jacket and gave it to her.

After the war she continued working in the intelligence services and spent some time in Russia but I never found out what she was doing there! Eventually she gave up her secret agent duties and just carried on as a midwife and community nurse. Margaret kept her Colt right up until the late 1970's when she decided that her eyesight was not as sharp as it should have been and she didn't want to shoot one of the girls from her local WI.

In her final years she kept the Westham community going with her enthusiasm and encouragement. When the vicar at St Marys (who seemed to have upset most of the parish before his retirement) locked the bell ringers out of the bell tower, locals say his next step was to dissolve the choir where Margaret was choirmaster. However he never did it. Gossip was that he dare not cross Margaret just in case he met with a sudden unexplained demise!

Margaret died in June of 2014 aged 94 and the locals came out of their houses en-masse, lining the High Street as the procession went by to the church.

It is a sobering thought that Margaret Spencer was the only one out of her SIS class that survived the war, and that was probably as much to do with luck as anything else! In the end my best memory of Margaret is one that she gave us all; the image of a nun floating down from the night sky with her habit tucked into her knickers. It always makes me smile.

From Westham I took the seafront road to my next call at East Dean and lapped up the perfect day. The promenade was heaving as everyone had come out to enjoy the weather. Gardeners were replanting the fabulous Carpet Gardens along by the pier and the coffee shops were doing a bustling trade.

I took the winding hill road towards the top of the Downs. The trees had joined at their tips to form a tunnel of green with sunlight bursting through. I carried on towards East Dean via Beachy Head. The warmth of the morning on the damp soil had made the flowers and herbs smell heavenly and the air by Black Robin Farm was filled with the sweet scent of camomile. The cow parsley was high and the orchids were in full bloom. The wind was pulsating through the long grass, sending ripples across the pastureland and high above me the skylarks were in full voice. They always sing louder in a good breeze.

It is difficult to put into words how breath taking the scenery can be at Beachy Head, in almost all weathers. These scenes have probably not changed much since ancient man cleared the hills for grazing thousands of years ago. Long may they last so that others can feel the utter joy that pours into the soul on these open grasslands.

Late at night during May and June the glow bugs would be sending out their signals looking for mates in the long grasses. The Snakes Head fritillaries were also in bloom and folklore tells that the first plants sprung up after the Romans invaded Britain. The plants spread with the legions across the country. Apparently, the tiny seeds were brought from the continent, wedged in the soldiers' boots.

Interestingly, some of the Downland herbs also came from the strangest of beginnings. Apparently long ago when monasteries and convents dotted the country their herb gardens were a closely guarded secret as they earned good money from selling their herbs and potions. High walled gardens protected their valuable plants but after the Dissolution of the Monasteries the high brick and stone walls were shattered. Come autumn when the seeds took to the winds, herbs self-seeded along the downland, becoming a common sight. I wonder if that gave rise to witches, who like the monks and priests used the ancient herbs to heal, or otherwise?

The day was just too beautiful to miss so at the highest point of the Downs I parked up for a quick break. I had an uninterrupted view eastward along the curving coastline towards Hastings, then to Dungeness beyond. To the west I could see Brighton stretching out into Worthing. In all, over 80 miles of stunning coastline and downland. I was on a patch of heaven with views only halted by the curving earth. This ancient land with its sensuous curving hills cut by silver rivers and sea has been shaped by humans since the end of the last Ice Age and has the ability to soothe the soul. It does not matter if you are wound like a lorry spring, a few minutes sitting somewhere along the crest of the Downs completely relaxes you. It has inspired so many writers and poets and someone once told me that William Blake wrote Jerusalem after visiting the unique chalk hills of our spectacular South Downs.

In the distance I could see an enormous dark cloud approaching. The spectacular panoramic views over the downland were made even more impressive by the distinct light and shade that was casting a patchwork of shadows over the fields and the sheep grazing below. The bitter winter winds of the last few months had made for a late spring but that had also kept the flowers in bloom for much longer and the cowslips and buttercups blended in to the fields of bright yellow rapeseed or mustard flowers (I can never tell the difference). They in turn contrasted spectacularly with the deep green of the silage grass grown for animal feed. A low rumbling thunder mixed with the song of the skylark as Beachy Head fell under the spell of Mother Nature.

Shafts of light broke through the darkest points in the cloud, creating hazy beams and I could see the heavy rain coming. The raincloud ominously moved over the car and for about three minutes the most amazingly noisy downpour took place. The cloud then carried on to Eastbourne. As the skies cleared above me the sun caught the rain and the finest rainbow I had seen for years lit up the grey backdrop, each curving colour distinct and bright. I could imagine all the sun seekers out for a stroll along the prom running for cover. I had to laugh as one end of the rainbow was out at sea but the closest end was smack on the pier, lighting it up in a golden haze. Sheikh Abid Gulzar, the new owner of the pier, would have been so happy to see it, confirming his dream that there really was a pot of gold to be had from our pier, big enough even to match the gold plated 700 horsepower supercar that he rumbles around town in.

With rainwater from the mini flash flood sheeting along the road I sparked the old girl. I sedately drove, around the hairpin bends and onward, passed Belle Tout Lighthouse towards East Dean. I remembered how I used to take the bends as a reckless teenager on my motorbikes, often at breakneck speed, sometimes even veering up the high grass banks as I screeched round. Now as an old man in an old banger I just took my time and ambled along, passed the lighthouse towards Birling Gap.

By the time I got to the curving low flint walls of Birling Manor the road was steaming in the heat. No one tucked inside their warm cosy offices would have ever guessed what had just happened.

The freshly repainted lighthouse sitting in a silver sea is an idyllic scene
and the Seven Sisters have to be the eighth wonder of the world.

I spotted Jimmy from the manor walking through the wet grass with his two dogs, a small brown border terrier and his faithful deaf old spaniel. As always Jimmy was casually dressed like a typical farm worker all in browns and greens, with worn cord trousers and an old wax coat. Over the years I had talked to Jimmy many times, yet in reality I hardly knew him. He was one of the handymen that the manor employed. Once he showed me around the 15th century manor and we chatted about the old inhabitants and their different building techniques that had left an indelible mark on the property and gardens.

Nearly 30 years ago the owners of Birling Manor decided to try

Both my trusty old bangers outside Birling Manor, one on call and the other for a friend's wedding. (See next page.)

holding weddings to help towards the running costs of the huge estate. My brother Sam was one of their first customers. Jimmy has never forgotten Sam's typical showy style, when a helicopter buzzed down from the sky and whisked him and his new bride away for their honeymoon. Sam's wedding was handled so successfully that it induced the estate to continue with weddings and all these years later we still attend the odd one there.

I pipped the horn and waved to him. He lifted the old piece of branch he was carrying and waved back. I doubt if he knew it was me but he was always friendly.

Birling Manor Estate has a fulltime specialist bricklayer on their books just to keep the miles of Sussex flint walls repaired. Some of the walls deteriorate on their own but some are helped along by reckless drivers who regularly plough through them on the sharp bends. You can see by the patchwork of new and old walls just how many accidents have happened along the stretch towards East Dean. Once I saw a Fiat upside down in one of the estate trees. Jimmy later told me that amazingly, after ploughing through the wall and flying through the air, the tree had caught the car like a ball in a catcher's mitt and both the occupants survived with hardly a scratch.

Jimmy is a quietly spoken unassuming and friendly chap. I often spot him pottering around the estate. It was only after years of knowing, but not knowing him, if you know what I mean, that I was told that he was actually the Lord of the Manor!

As I rounded the last bend before the straight to East Dean I spotted Beck up on the hillside with a lamb tucked under each arm. She was being followed down the hill by at least fifty other bleating balls of fluff, all leaping and bouncing along trying to get close to her. Beck runs the Seven Sisters Sheep Centre and her animals adore her.

Sadly I remembered as I waved to her that 2016 was to be her last season at the centre as she had decided that she needed a break after the 2.00am feeds and 24hr a day work. It wouldn't be the same when she stopped as it was always enjoyable spotting her blonde hair waving in the sun out in the middle of nowhere as she tended to her flock. Beck had actually been in finance before coming to run the farm and it must have been a real shock to move from being one of the high flyers up in the capital to a shepherd in our little corner of Sussex.

At my call in East Dean I couldn't find the address and when I phoned the old woman I was told how to get to her back garden gate. Lost again I phoned her for further instructions, and after

Helping out with the midnight feeding at the Seven Sister Sheep Centre. It is about 12.30am and amazing how hungry lambs are all day and night. Feeding the youngsters through the night is essential if they have no mothers. Its messy work but greatly rewarding and I loved it.

more searching and a short walk I was confronted with the large blue door down a small lane, exactly as she had described. The only problem was that it was locked! I rang her again but she told me that she had unlocked it and it was probably just stiff from the rain. I could hear in her voice that she was getting a bit fed up with me and started to talk loud and slow as if I was an idiot.

Being an expert on doors and gates, I mean I've opened countless thousands of them, I decided to have a go at opening it without any help. I hung up and wobbled the door again and I could clearly hear the bolts hitting, so I knew it was definitely locked. I deal with lots of old customers and the one thing that I have learnt is that you have to be patient and she was obviously mistaken (remember I am the self-proclaimed expert here). So I stood on my toolbox and reached over the top of the door and I felt a large bolt. With a little effort I managed to slide it across and carefully clambered back down to open the door, but it wouldn't budge. With a little more wobbling I could hear there was another bolt further down the door.

I needed to get much higher so that I could lean right over to the lower bolt. Once more I clambered up onto my toolbox, then scrambled further up onto the overgrown fence. I managed to get a good foot hold, high on the gate. It was tricky as everything was still wet and one slip would see me sitting on my backside in the mud. I looked over and spotted the second bolt just below the door handle. I leaned over as much as I could but I was still a few inches short. I shouted "Hello" a few times but could hear nothing. The back of the house was hidden by the long garden and there was no signs of life. I got back down and wondered what to do. I was so close but so far.

I had rung my customer three times already and I was definitely appearing to be the village idiot to her. I needed to take the initiative and sort this out. I looked around for a stick but there was nothing to hand and then I spotted my leather work book by my tool box. I pushed the workbook up into the hedge and once more ascended. Grabbing the book and leaning over the top of the door as much as possible without toppling, I started to manipulate the lower bolt. Slowly it moved across.

It was hard going, bent over the door frame (luckily I have ample padding) but with my feet dangling in the air I could just reach the bolt and not overbalance. Bit by bit the bolt jiggled back until it just cleared. I felt a flush of joy, like a safe-cracker when the safe clicks open but it was short-lived. I heard a sound that sent a shiver down my spine; a deep rattling bark. I looked up to see a stocky brown, short-haired dog with black jagged stripes, charging at full pace towards me. It looked like a small pit bull and its paws were actually banging the grass like a drum as it ran. My eyes widened in panic as I tried to shuffle my weight back over the door frame so that I wouldn't fall forward into its slobbering jaws. Just as the dog reached me I managed to move my position but it leapt up, bouncing against the door and its jaws locked onto my leather work book. In that folder was all my important documents; invoice books, customers details, everything I needed and I wasn't going to let 'Fangs' eat it. I pulled as hard as I could without falling into the garden and it pulled back, snarling and growling, staring straight into my eyes like a demented demon. It was at this point when you think things can't get any worse, it did.

In all the commotion, growling, snarling and dribbling, me shouting and general panic, I heard another spine chilling sound, a click! It was so loud that both me and the dog momentarily stopped as we both realised it was the door catch clicking open. The door creaked a little and then started to swing ajar. I was dead for sure. I could just see the epitaph on my grave, 'Sewing machine specialist, eaten for breakfast.'

Suddenly I felt something attack my legs. I had no idea that it was my saviour who had arrived in the shape of a small skinny woman coming up from behind and pulling me to safety. She pulled me with such force that I let go of my workbook and dropped to the floor. She then pushed open the gate and shouted (in a surprisingly loud voice for her size) "POPPY, POPPY SIT!" Suddenly the devil dog (with the girly name) stopped in its tracks and transformed into an obedient mutt. It sat and wagged its tail. I cautiously walked up to Poppy and gently tried to pull my work book out of her mouth. She growled but the woman shouted again and Poppy dropped it. I picked it up, noticing a neat row of marks from the dog's teeth and slobber everywhere. I was slowly backing away when her owner came running down the garden. She attached a lead to the dog and exchanged a few pleasantries with the old dear, ignoring me completely. She then threw a glance my way that could turn a man to stone and shoved me out of her garden, slamming the door in my face. I heard the bolts that I had just spent ages undoing 'clunk' back into position and turned to see the old dear shaking her head behind me.

"You're here to fix my sewing machine I assume?" Said the skinny woman who was obviously the customer I had rang three times earlier.
"Er, this isn't your house then?"
"No. Mine is the blue door just there," she said, pointing to another near identical door, a few yards further along the path.

"No one tries to get into Belinda's garden, not with that dog and her door double-locked! Chop chop, come along now. I have a WI meeting in less than an hour, no time to dilly-dally."

I brushed myself off, picked up my toolbox, and sheepishly waddled along behind her, just like the village idiot that she had suspected I was all along!

MAD DOGS & ENGLISHMEN

"My mum says she knew you were coming, she jus' forgot to get up! My mum says you should come in and fix her machine. My mum says she's going to make us breakfast. I'm 'avin' porridge and my bear is 'avin' some too. I bet mum makes you porridge." A face as bright as sunrise was beaming up at me from the front door. The lad, around four or five, was still in his Star Wars pyjamas. Under his bright golden curls was a mass of freckles and a smile like a row of stacked bricks on a building site. He was clutching a raggy old bear that had obviously been the brunt of many adventures and next to him sat a golden retriever staring at the events unfolding.

"I'm Alex, what's your name?" I asked.

"Mafew, but mum jus' calls me Trouble. My bear's Tubby and he's Mac," he said putting his arm around the dog and giving him a big hug. "I can show you where the machine is – after you've fixed it we're going to make new clothes for Tubby today. Tubby broke it," then quietly added, "It was me really, I tried to fix Tubby's ear and now it won't work at all. Don't tell mum will you?"

"Of course not," I smiled, "It will be our secret."

Sometime later, after a lot of clanging, banging, and footsteps running here and there I heard the delightful sound of a Nespresso machine hiss into life. Moments later a pretty young mother, with her hair all in tangles rushed in with a cup of coffee for me. "Marge next door told me you like two sugars."

"Sure do" I replied, beaming more at the coffee than her. "Nothing starts my day better than a good cup of Java, and this week the papers are saying that it's apparently good for you! Oh, I found this piece of toast stuck in the bobbin winder, heaven only knows what your son was up to!"

"He was trying to fix Tubby's ear," She answered back with a grin. "He thinks I don't know but it was obvious with all his little finger marks everywhere and half of Tubby's ear still in the machine. Last week we caught him discussing, very seriously, with his school friend Max how to make waistcoats for one of Max's ferrets. I'm sure he's going to be a designer when he grows up. If I don't strangle him first!"

"Waistcoats for ferrets are not as mad as you think. I have a machinist in Brighton who has made a business out of that for years, Doris even has a busy website called Ferret Couture."

Before long I had left the pandemonium of the household and was sitting in traffic trying to get through Alfriston to my next call at a manor on the outskirts. Alfriston has one road in and out. In recent years, with the population explosion, a million cars try to get down a street made for a horse and cart. During rush hour everything grinds to a halt. I edged slowly forward as one car after another managed to squeeze through, but we came to a grinding halt opposite the Smugglers pub.

It was standing outside that very place years ago that I had one of those revelation moments that we all have. It was a summer's day and I was leaning against a warm brick wall while my wife posted a parcel in the Post Office. I was thinking how amazing it was that energy from the sun, all the way across the universe could be heating the very wall that I was leaning on. It seemed impossible but thankfully that's how it all works. Then it hit me. I knew from my old science teacher Mr Cousins at St Bede's, that energy cannot be destroyed; not ever. It can be transformed but never destroyed. So what if that answers the age old question about ghosts? I'll explain my crazy theory. If a brick can absorb energy from across the endless vastness of space, why can't it absorb our energy? What if ghosts are really no more than an area that has absorbed the energy from an incident? Then, when all the climatic elements are just right it is released again, creating what we mistakenly call ghosts, just like the brick wall was releasing the heat from the sun. All it needs is for the area to have remained much the same since whatever happened, happened. It may also explain why ghosts seem to inhabit older, unchanged areas. All a ghost may be is absorbed energy being released. The more dramatic the event, the more energy is absorbed by the surrounding area, then the area sits there until that dark misty night when all the elements are just perfect and releases. Well that's my theory anyway, and until Stephen Hawking disproves it, I'm sticking to it.

Eventually, after getting completely confused by my customer's directions, I arrived down a gravel drive to a smart farmhouse come manor. I parked next to a new Range Rover, a two-tone mini Clubman and a beautiful 1960's Mercedes open top tourer. The whole place looked like it had just jumped out of the pages of Country Life magazine.

I was shown to the sewing machine sitting on a grand mahogany table next to a large window overlooking the back garden. Behind the machine was a beautiful but unfinished patchwork quilt ready to be completed, once the machine was running again. Glancing outside I noticed a weird statue in the middle of the lawn being held up by a pole. I didn't pay too much attention to it at first but there was something wrong with the picture and I kept looking up from my work trying to figure out what it was. However I was staring into the sun and I couldn't see that clearly.

When the lady of the house returned to see how I was doing I asked her about the statue. "Oh that's no statue. That is my idiot of a husband!"
"What! But he hasn't moved and I've been here nearly half an hour. What on earth is he up to?"
"He is waiting for a mole! If you look closely you can see his footsteps in the dew where he crept up to the mole hill just before sunrise this morning." She was right, just visible was a small path leading to what I thought was a statue. "So what is that pole he's holding?"
"That's no pole, it's his shotgun pointed down at the lawn. He has decided that after trying to trap the mole for months that he would blow it into oblivion. You can't see because we are looking into the light, but he has got a pair of hearing aids in his ears that he bought from Spec Savers. He's a golfer you see, and loves his flat lawn with perfect stripes. One of his golfing buddies came up with the stupid idea during one of their club days. Apparently he saw it somewhere and it's supposed to work. What the idiot's doing is listening for the digging of the mole. He's learnt that the

mole sometimes comes past just after dawn. For the last week he has set our alarm and been out there every morning, waiting for him."

"Mad dogs and Englishmen!" I laughed

"I often wonder if he loves that piece of grass more than me. You know he carries a small pair of scissors in his pocket and I have seen him reach down and clip bits of grass during his daily inspections. What you are looking at is 15 years of obsessive work. The only fly in his perfect ointment is the mole. I think I am falling in love with it. All his grand plans for a perfect lawn to show off to his golfing cronies are being blown to the wind by my little four-legged friend, who I might add, has outsmarted him time and time again, it's driving him mad and making me a happy woman. When he was up in the city he ran a large corporation and always got his own way. He is a bit of a control freak, but now he has found an enemy who does not bow to his will. It's driving him crazy and fulfilling my life. Every night I raise my glass to that little creature and quietly toast my beautiful mole hills."

Sometime later I was just putting the finishing touches to the sewing machine and there was an almighty KERUUMPF! Startled I looked up to see a small mushroom cloud above the husband. His wife came running in and we both started out of the window. As the smoke cleared, just yards behind the husband, a mole crept out of the lawn and made a dash for the undergrowth, its shiny fur catching the sun as it scurried away to safety. The husband was oblivious of its escape. He was too busy trying to brush the muck off him from his shotgun blast. We both looked at each other and burst out laughing.

Moments later the back door crashed open and in fell the husband with the biggest grin on his muddy face. I noticed that he even had mud in his teeth. "Got the bugger dear. Dead as a door nail or my name's Nelly." The husband then leant his shotgun against the fireplace and went to shake his Barbour coat outside the back door. Amazingly, under his coat he was wearing a pair of very expensive Paisley Print crimson silk pyjamas! He turned and saw me and for a moment looked a little bemused, but his wife explained and he introduced himself with an enthusiastic handshake. "Sorry for the noise old boy, been after that blasted mole for ages, crafty little sod. I've used traps, poison, even sonic deterrents. Nothing worked until now. He won't be bothering me anymore. Ha, blasted to kingdom come." He laughed as he turned and walked towards the other room, adding to his wife, "Got to phone Charlie at the club and let him know the mole is history."

"Yes dear," came her reply.

As soon as he had left the room she whispered to me, "Don't tell him the mole has escaped. Let him have his day of glory. We're shopping in Brighton later and I'm sure I'll get at least one new pair of shoes out of him. Possibly lunch too!"

As I left, my customer smiled and said cheekily, "Don't forget to wave to 'Nelly' as you go by." I got her joke immediately and had the impression she was going to have a great day. The husband was by the hole that he had shot into his lawn. Next to him was a wheelbarrow, spade and a grass roller. He was just so happy and was singing away to himself in the morning air louder than a drunken vicar at a pub social. "MORNING HAS BROKEN LIKE THE FIRST MOOORNING, BLACKBIRD HAS SPOKEN LIKE THE FIRST BIIIRD." He picked up his spade and waved to me as I rumbled by. I smiled and waved back, smothering my instinct to burst into laughter again. I could just imagine that little mole digging a new hole and making his way back to the lawn, pushing up a few more hills as he went. And even funnier, the uncontrollable rage when the hubby opened his curtains to see them!

As I drove away from Alfriston, in much easier traffic, it suddenly hit me that the husband had been singing the very song that we had sung as kids in school assembly, and Cat Stevens had made his own. Interestingly, residents of Alfriston proudly say that the poem words were originally commissioned by a local vicar who was also the editor of Songs of Praise magazine. He'd asked Eleanor Farjeon, a famous children's author, (who was staying locally at a friend's house in the early 1930's) to write a poem about the beauty of creation that could be put to an old tune. And so 'Morning Has Broken' was born.

From Alfriston I made my way up the Sussex lanes to a corset makers. They had nearly gone out of business a few years back but being in close proximity to Brighton they had found a new source of revenue. It had come from an unlikely source, like the lorry driver who liked to wear corsets when not at work and a few others like him. With prices starting at over £500 they were beautifully made, just a little wider than they used to be to fit their new clientele!

Later in the morning I passed Bede's Senior School at Upper Dicker on my way to Eagle E-Types. The old manor was built by the Liberal MP and scoundrel Horatio Bottomley, who had so much power that it is said he even had a railway station built, just down the road at Berwick so that the London train could stop and pick him up. I have written about him before in my books and he is a fascinating creature.

Politicians come in all shapes and sizes and none were more devious than Bottomley. He holds the title of possibly the most audacious fraudster in British political history. Bottomley was born in 1860 and grew up in an orphanage in London's East End. He was as hard as nails and as cunning as a fox. He had a brilliant legal mind and moved fast. By the age of twenty eight he had founded the Financial Times and a few years later he became a Member of Parliament.

By the outbreak of the First World War he was fabulously wealthy and had come up with a scheme to make himself even richer. He started the John Bull Victory Bond Club, basically a savings scheme for people to invest in, with the added bonus of monthly cash prizes. He toured the Western Front and gave great crowd pleasing speeches to the masses. The funds in his club grew and grew. Along with his weekly 'John Bull' publication (which sold over two million copies a week), he amassed a second fortune.

Sitting on a pot of gold it was not long before his weak will and greed got the better of him. He started to embezzle the hard saved cash from the poor communities and used it to build and maintain his grand houses and lifestyle. It all came crashing down when he was caught and sent to prison. He lost everything and when he was released he made a meagre living performing a one-man act on stage. It was during one of these performances at London's Windmill Theatre in 1933 that he collapsed and died.

There were very few soft words in the periodicals of the day when Bottomley died but on the plus side he did build some amazing places. Bede's survives as a reminder to all of us that life is a slippery pole and it can take no time at all to slide all the way from the dizzy heights down to the gutter.

By midday I was being given the 'ten bob tour' by Matt, one of the directors of Eagle E-Types, in Hadlow Down. They have the

Here I am in the fabulous upholstery workshop of Eagle E-Types. The pleasure of fixing an upholstery machine that is working on high-end supple leather for millionaires cars is unique. In the foreground is an E-Type under restoration. Don't tell them but I would probably do their machines for free if they asked, just to have another tour of their premises.

most pristine workshops I have ever seen and build special Jaguars for special people. Some say it is the finest specialist engineering works of its kind in the world. While I was there they had just finished an E-type costing over a million pounds, which apparently Jeremy Clarkson was due to test drive. In the upholstery room I worked on the leather machine as the upholsterer, another Alex, refitted the boot of an E-Type. That beauty was selling at a mere £450,000.

As I left I let Matt know which three I would like to buy with my lottery winnings at the weekend. When I reversed out of my driving space I saw that my 20yr old Discovery had left a little oil patch on their pristine paving. I whipped off quickly before anyone saw it, telling her to take more care next time, the mucky pup.

From Hadlow Down I made my way along to Warbleton where I had a call near the Black Duck Pub, opposite the medieval church of St Mary the Virgin.

Warbleton Church has a fascinating plaque inside dedicated to Richard Woodman, a young Sussex farmer and ironmaster. Richard was a Protestant martyr during the reign of 'Bloody Mary', and the plaque tells his sorry tale. Richard had outspoken views that led to a warrant being issued for his arrest. When the arresting officers came for him he leapt out of his farm window and made a run for it up a path to the woods. He was a fit young farmer running barefoot for his life. The men chasing him were in full uniform and weighed down with equipment so had little hope of catching him. Unfortunately when he was running he made the cardinal mistake, as per all horror B-movies; he looked back to see how close his chasers were. That simple action was to cost him his life. When he turned he trod into a hole and twisted his ankle. Injured and hobbling they caught up with him and dragged him away for cross-examination. Eventually after

Richard Woodman's memorial stone.

299

> IN THE VAULTS BENEATH
> THIS BUILDING WERE
> IMPRISONED TEN OF THE
> SEVENTEEN PROTESTANT
> MARTYRS WHO WERE
> BURNED AT THE STAKE
> WITHIN A FEW YARDS
> OF THIS SITE 1555-1557
> THEIR NAMES ARE RECORDED
> ON THE MEMORIAL TO BE
> SEEN ON CLIFFE HILL
>
> "FAITHFUL UNTO DEATH"

The Sussex Martyrs and the plaque on Lewes Town Hall to commemorate the poor souls who died for their religious beliefs. It seems impossible today to think that in Britain you could once be killed for a few loose words. Heavens knows what they would have thought of Twitter and Facebook!

thirty two 'examinations' he was taken to Lewes. In the June of 1557 he was burnt at the stake with nine others (including four women) outside the Star Inn, which is now the Town Hall.

You may wonder what terrible crime he committed to warrant such a horrendous punishment. His crime was to argue with the local vicar, who one year was preaching Protestant views, and the next Roman Catholic. "You're turning your preaching from head to tail," Richard had told him. That one sentence shouted at Rector Fairbanke signed his death warrant. In the reign of Bloody Mary, where intolerance and persecution was commonplace, a simple slip of the tongue could cost you your life.

Richard is known as one of the Sussex Martyrs and he is regularly celebrated in Lewes on bonfire night. In that strange way that fate has, if he had not twisted his ankle he would probably have escaped into the woods and today no one would have ever known that he existed.

I often think when I am driving along, that hidden in the folds of the Sussex Weald are fascinating droplets of our past, and every now and again they trickle out before your very eyes.

After the pub (and timely refuelling with a superb pie and chips) I hit the road for Hastings. I took Barley Mow Lane up to Punnett's Town and then the Dallington Road to Netherfield and the wiggly back road to John's Cross. From John's Cross I hit the A21, Vinehall Road to Kent Street and Ebden's Hill, noting as I went all the houses and workshops that I had called on over the years. Within forty minutes I was rolling down St Helen's Road into the centre of Hastings.

Normally I would not make such a large leap in one day but my last call at Hastings was an emergency at Bustles & Bows, the wedding dress and prom dress supplier in the High Street. As with all emergencies the machine had gone wrong at the worst time. It had jammed with the wedding dress still stuck in the machine and in a few days it was the last fitting before the wedding.

For all its faults you can't help loving Hastings. It is one of the most fascinating mixtures of architecture, culture and history that you will find in any British town.

Out of all the famous people who have come out of Hastings my all-time favourite character lived just up the road from the High Street and was called Archie Belaney or as the world knew him, Grey Owl, the Hastings Indian. I am going to finish this story, not with my usual sewing machine travels, but with one of my fallen heroes.

Archie was born in 1888 and grew up with his grandmother and two aunts at 36 St Mary's Terrace, a narrow road cut high into the Sussex chalk, just along from the ancient castle. The row of terraced houses have a wonderful view over part of Hastings and more importantly they were not far from St Helen's Park and Fairlight Glenn, now part of a nature reserve. At the end of his road was the old smugglers caves and panoramic views over the sea from the castle ruins. This combination of wild heaven was the perfect recipe for a young lad and fuelled his dreams of adventure.

Archie had grown up in a broken home and had become a loner,

Archie Belaney, Grey Owl, was a dreamer who made his dream come true.

The former house of the Hastings Indian in St Mary's Terrace. It is hard to believe that Archie went on to entertain royalty and cause a worldwide sensation.

making his own life one of escapism, probably to help him cope with his situation. He would often disappear into the woods, tracking the local wildlife, making tools, weapons and makeshift camps. Archie may have been a solitary boy but he was as bright as a button and earned a place at William Parker Academy, a sort of early grammar school, where, much to his classes' amusement, he would mimic the sounds of the wild animals that he had seen in the woods.

I have absolutely no doubt that when Buffalo Bill and his troupe toured Britain, Archie would have gone to see him in Hastings and probably a few of the other towns as well as they journeyed around the country in 1902, 1903 and 1904. He would have been at the perfect age to be completely intoxicated with the amazing showman and his fabulous travelling entourage. I would bet you a week's worth of coffee and cake that Archie would have hopped onto the Hastings train and headed for Eastbourne on the 19th August 1903, where Colonel Cody was appearing in person near the Crumbles Bridge along Seaside in Eastbourne. A gigantic arena was set up so that the Deadwood Stage could come hurtling in, attacked by whooping Indians. Over 700 men worked for Buffalo Bill and 500 horses were needed for his Wild West Spectacular. There were two performances, the later evening performance being under 'brilliant new illuminations' supplied by the latest wonder of the age, electric lighting.

As Archie grew it became clear that he was very different to the other boys and when he was still a kid he tried to talk his long suffering grandmother into paying for him to go to study in Canada. I can guess that he knew as soon as he was there he was going to go native. She struck a deal with Archie; if he promised to study well and took a job as soon as he was old enough, she in turn would agree to pay his passage to study in the last great frontier of Canada when he turned twenty.
However, Archie was a little too impatient and after leaving school he hated his new job at the wood store with such venom,

that one night he climbed onto the roof, lowered a tub of gunpowder down the chimney and blew the place up!

To avoid jail, Archie was quickly rushed off to Liverpool and took a steamer to Canada. He loved Canada, it was his dream come true. However it all went pear shaped for a few years and during this time Archie became a womanising drunk, a liar, cheat, and the lowest of the low. As time went by Archie had a million amazing adventures in Canada and even returned to Hastings to see his relatives while he was in Europe fighting as a sniper in the First World War. After he was wounded he took up with a local girl that he had known as a kid and married her. Unfortunately for her, Archie may also have had another wife in Canada, maybe even two!

It was not long before Archie became restless and disappeared back to Canada where he became an accomplished trapper, earning his living trading beaver skins and furs. While spending his life in the wilderness he slowly transformed from the Hastings boy into a wild Canadian.

This is where it gets fascinating. Archie, or Grey Owl as he had become, had seen the demise of many of Canada's wild animals, especially the beaver, which was so sought after by exclusive hat makers for its soft and silky waterproof skin. Trade in animal pelts helped the Canadian economy boom, even geese were hunted for their feathers that made great quill pens! As more and more animals were hunted Archie became aware that the stunning Canadian wilderness he loved so dearly was becoming a wasteland.

It was on one his many trapping trips that something profoundly changed in him. While trapping and skinning he came across two orphaned beaver cubs (he had probably trapped and killed the adults). Instead of killing them he took the pair in and raised them as his own. This is the point where Archie changed from killer to conservationist.

Archie spent years in the wild and with his excellent schooling Archie was able to describe his travels and adventures with his beaver cubs. During the long cold winters Archie scribbled his escapades down and then sent them to a publisher in England. Sussex Life started to publish the stunning articles from the tall, dark Indian (by now Archie Belaney had made the complete transformation from Sussex schoolboy to Grey Owl, First Nation Indian). Unlike John Muir, one of the first famous naturalists, Archie had taken on a new persona and hid behind it.

Archie became the wild frontiersman he wrote about. It is as if he believed his own made-up story that he was a true Indian. He told people that his father was a scout and personal friend of Buffalo Bill's and his mother was an Apache! As his writing grew more and more popular in the 1930's, he went from small publications to complete books. Some of his publications, like Men of the Last Frontier, Pilgrims of the Wild, and The Vanishing Frontier, were best sellers. Readers found it the perfect escapism from the depression era of the 1930's as, in spirit, they joined Grey Owl on his real life adventures.

Few suspected that Grey Owl was anything other than what he appeared to be, the perfect frontier Indian. As his fame grew he started to give lectures and his one-man tours became so popular that he sold out every venue. When he toured Britain on his first tour, over a quarter of a million people flocked to see the exotic stranger from a faraway land tell tales of hunting amongst the tall pines of the distant wilderness. Grey Owl's success also secured publicity for his passion to protect the beaver and he became instrumental in the setting up of National Parks where the beaver could flourish without persecution.

His next tour was even more popular and police were needed for crowd control. However all this pressure was taking its toll on Archie's health. By the time he was 50 it all caught up with him. In 1938 he went back to his little cabin, Beaver Lodge, on the shore of Ajawaan Lake in the Canadian woods, and just faded away, a sad and lonely figure. He was discovered on his cabin floor and taken to hospital, but it was too late. Officially they say he died of pneumonia but people that knew him said that he basically died of loneliness and exhaustion.

However Archie's story was not over because the press found out that Grey Owl, the great Canadian Indian conservationist, the impassioned son of an Apache who had entertained royalty was none other than a fraud, a trickster, a bigamist and a runaway school boy from Hastings. The story was sensational and made press around the world.

The tabloids ignored all the amazing conservation works and writings of Grey Owl and went for the throat. They had a field day as they branded him a cheat and a liar, bringing up all his wives and women, breaking down his carefully built façade as an Indian. Some short-sighted libraries even took his books off the shelves, missing the whole point of what the little schoolboy had tried to accomplish.

Archibald Belaney was born a tortured soul. As a boy he had a crazy dream, but unlike most of us, he made that dream a reality. Today, conservation is part of our lives but it was because of men like Archie that it all started. In reality he accomplished great things that led to a better world for all of us. His writing is spectacular and gives us an insight into a lost frontier; a frontier where no white man had stepped, where the beaver and elk roamed free from persecution and where a pristine wilderness flourished.

Archie was a deeply flawed human being, but with that said he was also a hero, a passionate man and great ambassador for his cause, who ultimately ended up dying for what he believed in.

Today, in hindsight, we are more forgiving of his wayward ways and his conservation work is greatly admired. My favourite James Bond actor, Pierce Brosnan, played Grey Owl in a film with the same name and it gives a little insight into his troubled character.

His grave is by his lodge next to Ajawaan Lake in Prince Albert National Park. It is marked with a simple cross. On the horizontal bar it reads Archie Belaney, on the downward post it reads Grey Owl. If there was one man that I would love to spend a day with (besides my dad) it would be my local hero, Archie Belaney from 36 St Mary's Terrace. Our very own Hastings Indian.

Last Man Standing

"We have something in common, who would have believed it!" Shouted a small, round man in a sudden fit of excitement. I was on my way out of the door after servicing a quilting machine when a consultant surgeon had accosted me in his hallway. I'm pretty sure that he glided across the floor over to me, in that self-important manner that many consultants have perfected. On my way in to fix his wife's machine he hadn't even bothered to look up from his computer, but now, after hearing what his wife had said he sprang into action.

We were face to face. "Yes, yes," he articulated, throwing his arms up as he spoke. "I spend hours bringing back a patient from near death, I do everything perfectly to save their life. When they eventually sit up the first thing they say is that they hope they never see me again! It hurts, you know."
"I'm used to it after all these years" I said, laughing. I knew what she had meant by it and it was nothing nasty. I had been quite accustomed to this final parting and for many customers I never do see them again so sometimes it is true.

Actually my trade had been declining for years and I often thought of myself a little like the tinker, tailor and candlestick maker; on the way out! It was not surprising, over the decades I had been in the middle of the greatest decline in British history, the decline of manufacturing. Britain had started the Industrial Revolution and in my life it was not man walking on the moon or the first computer that I witnessed first-hand but the amazing loss of powerhouse Britain.

As a kid in the 1960's, Britain was booming and we made just about everything we needed. The drab 1940's had trundled into the 1950's and as the last rationing came to an end Rock'n'Roll blew the old cobwebs away, Mantovani was suddenly moved along by Elvis, Jerry Lee Lewis and Teddy Boys. Britain basked in a new gyrating freedom, never seen before.

However, global competition meant that British manufacturing was disappearing as fast as snow in summer. Towns like Luton had over 100,000 people employed in the hat industry, Nottingham had even more in lace making. Factories darkened our skies as we became the stuff of nightmares and dark satanic mills. Amazingly today only a handful of these great industries struggle on.

In my area alone there were hundreds of factories and in my books I have gone into some detail about their great products. With all these factories came the skilled engineers that maintained them and the highly skilled machinists who sweated away day by day.

When I was a fit young lad I had around thirty sewing machine engineers plying their trade around me. Some were good, some weren't, and I could usually tell who had been working on a machine before me by the way it was repaired, the scratches to the screw heads and how the machines stitched.

As manufacturing declined, one by one the sewing machine engineers faded away, retired or died but in my mind's eye I see them all. While the last vestiges of empire crumbled, several of them had helped me get started in the rag trade which was in its last gasps. As the decline of manufacturing continued at an unprecedented rate I was one of the happy few to survive. Let me tell you why.

As communications improved, along with shipping and containers, for the first time in history our world shrunk. Any budding entrepreneur in any country in the world could supply goods to any other.

Global capitalism arrived on my doorstep in 1987 in the shape of a small, round Chinese man in a tight suit. Under his arm was tucked the bestselling product of our family firm, a white Broderie Anglaise padded Moses basket. To cut, make and trim (CMT) that item was just over £29. Now, our entrepreneur showed us his product (that even had a flame proof mattress and puke holes in case the baby threw up). It was a beauty and better than our version, which we had supplied for years to many major retailers like Debenhams, John Lewis, and Harrods, (even via our specialists stockist, to a few of the young royals at the time). Then came the crunch. Our budding capitalist explained that he sold by the container load and if we bought half a container of fully dressed Moses baskets they would cost us, wait for it, just £2 each. Crazy eh! A product from the other side of the world could be made for less than what we paid for the trim on our baskets.

My brother Nik looked over to me and in his eyes I saw the end of our company. It took a few years but by 1990 I was up and running as Sussex Sewing Machines, Nik had disappeared to make his millions and the great family business that my parents had dreamed up in the 1950's slid down the tubes. Only my youngest brother, Olly, had the sense to farm off a small proportion of it and continue the old business name.

As things went pear-shaped in Britain we still struggled to compete and the pressure was extreme in almost every industry. Like I say I was happy to see the back of it as the last days of manufacturing on a large scale was a bloodbath. As the bosses tried to compete the first thing they did was cut wages, then increase working hours. Usually they tried to make savings in the product which led to cheaper products, but cheap in the wrong way. Returns mounted as shortcuts were taken and quality dropped. Then things got really nasty.

A perfect example was piecework. Piecework was a two-way deal between the bosses and the workers and millions of people in Britain relied on it. If the product was priced just right the worker made a living and the boss made enough profit to carry on. However wobble that boat (which had been in balance for decades) and everyone suffered.

The real monsters were the time and motion men (probably failed traffic wardens) who started making severe and unfair cuts, measuring each item, timing each action, looking how to make even more cuts from the already over pressurised workers. My dad had the right idea, he timed three women on a product and came up with a price. They then told him how much they wanted and a deal was struck. They were happy and he made money.

Jump to the 1980's and the final death knell of true mass production in Britain. Companies were closing at over a thousand a week. Businesses that had been going for generations were tumbling like wheat before the harvester.

The time and motion men became harsher and more devious. They started measuring the offcuts in the bin, measuring the time workers took to go to the loo. You think that's bad, it gets worse! It was all in vain as these old companies were not a level playing field and competition with emerging nations was truly impossible.

As the final battle came to an end and the last of the old traders died out in the 1990's, Britain had to look to the future, not in old traditional ways but in new and exciting trades. A few of the old school managed to hang on with royal warrants or other special abilities but the bulk of our old industries had gone. Luckily for me the rise of hobby sewing saved my bacon, as people learnt to see sewing as a pleasure not a chore.

The death knell in manufacturing came when the time and motion men discovered a new weapon, silence! They put listening devices around the machinist and workers. Each device listened to an individual. At the end of the working week they were called into the office and interrogated. "We have paid you for a 40 hour week including bonuses for piecework and hitting your targets."

"I always do my best sir."

"That is not quite true. Our listening devices have shown us that during your working week when we have paid you to sew there was 427 minutes silence when your machine was not earning money! When your machine is silent we are losing money as we are paying you for doing nothing. Accordingly we have deducted money from your wages."

This betrayal of the workforce was felt at every level in every area of the country from the shop floor to the office. As new trades and ideas sprung up I was glad to see the back of the old sweat shops where bad wages and even worse working environments flourished. I hated going into the old factories it was sometimes like stepping back into a dark tale from Charles Dickens.

Companies started to cheat me as they were cheating their workers. I would be called in to repair machines and then not paid. In one instance I had rented out machinery to a business in Eastbourne. After they failed to pay me for six months I went down to find the place empty! I lost everything. One business in Hastings called Hollywood Curtains had me service and set every sewing machine that they had and give them a written report stating so. That was on the Friday. When the girls came into work on the following Monday the gates were locked and a notice saying that the business had closed was pinned to the fence. Over the weekend the factory had been cleared. Selling fully serviced machines would get a far higher price so they had planned the whole thing. It was a rough time and I am glad to see the back of it.

The empty factories were flattened and new developments took their place. Britain slowly changed to a modern competitive country with innovative ideas and small efficient production units.

Today a lot of my customers are in businesses concentrating on niche markets where quality, style and innovation outweigh cheaper mass production. Of course Britain survived, but it was a different Britain and whatever people say regarding manufacturing, it is better now for us, the workers, than ever.

There are a few individual factories that I still look after, like Monsoon Automotive run by Michael Winterton. They have a factory along the Upper Dicker that makes car hoods and covers, one of only three specialists left in the country. The last time I was there an American Mustang was having a new convertible roof fabricated. It is a step back in time for me, the noise and excitement of good manufacturing. Sewing machines going off in short staccato bursts like machine gun fire as they join miles of fabric. The cutters are cutting, the fitters fitting, and loud music drowning out the lot. It is like a battlefield, action and noise everywhere. Workers shout messages out across the workroom floor (along with plenty of sign language) and the place buzzes with excitement. There are just a few manufacturing centres like this left in my area.

I was one of the survivors in my trade, more by luck than judgement. I was just a kid when it all started to crash. I rolled with it as the factories fell and sewing went from a badly paid trade to a wonderful hobby craft for enthusiasts. My old mentors have all faded away as well, and in my business, as the title tells, I became the last man standing.

I remember my dear old colleague, David Cowan bemoaning the destruction of manufacturing. Dave had taken over the upkeep of the sewing machines at our family business from Mr Peek. Peek had a sewing machine shop in Old Town, almost opposite The Tally Ho pub, at 45 Church Street, before it was compulsory purchased for road widening in the 1970's. He moved to Broderick Road next to the community centre and then to a little shop at 12 Susan's Road. My dad would phone him in desperation about an emergency breakdown (telephone number Eastbourne 631). Mr Peek would buzz round to our outworkers on his moped (funnily enough my only memory of him was that he always wore a small peeked helmet and smelt of two-stroke oil). Anyway, Dave Cowan had taken over from Mr Peek and he was one of the many skilled engineers who had taught me basic industrial sewing machine maintenance. Dave had come down from Blackburn in Lancashire, one of the true centres of textile manufacturing in our country. He used to tell me of the great mills and factory chimneys that filled the valley skylines, and the sounds of whistles and bells that filled the workers daily routines.

One factory that Dave worked in apparently had over 500 sewing girls in great sewing lines. The machines were powered by overhead shafts, which dropped belts down to each machine. When a belt broke, production was not allowed to stop and Dave would crawl underneath the sewing tables and make his way along the lines of machines (and women's legs) until he got to the broken belt. It was a tricky art, joining a belt and swinging it back onto the pulley mechanism without slowing production. In amongst all this noise and grime was humour and Dave used to tell me with a laugh that he always knew how far along the line he had crawled when he came upon the massive legs of Hairy Mary!

While a few modern textile factories still flourish in places like Leicester, Dave was one of the last of the engineers who had seen the old Northern powerhouses in all their grubby glory. He had come down and settled just about as far away from them as he could, down to the clean seaside air of Eastbourne. Initially he had found work at Alstons in Courtlands Road, but the corset makers were in their dying throes and soon disappeared (one more casualty amongst the millions).

Dave later opened up a little corner shop at 114 Seaside. Each day I would see him cycle along from his house, park his bike up and put on his brown work coat. He seemed to be the twin of Albert Arkwright, the character from that great sitcom Open All Hours. I can't remember him wearing a peaked cap but one would have suited him perfectly. He had a wide face and cheeky grin. Perched precariously on the very tip of his nose was his half-rim glasses that he would stare at you over.

Dave's shop was the centre of the world for people that sewed in Eastbourne. It was a jumble of countless parts and machines, ribbons and threads, zips and buttons. If there was something special you needed he would pop into his back room and reappear as if by magic holding the part you needed. Over the years I bought several of my favourite collectible machines from

David Cowan's corner shop was a treasure trove for all who sewed in Eastbourne and crammed to the ceiling with all kinds of wonderful sewing paraphernalia.

him. We would often drool over machines that neither of us could afford, advertised in antiques magazines – I miss him.

Yes, they are all gone now and so has the Britain that I had grown up in, the manufacturing thumping heart of our empire. Like I say, seeing its decline has been the most amazing thing that has happened to me in my lifetime. And the biggest surprise of all, as one of my clients recently announced, sewing is now cool!

*   *   *   *   *

Back at my customer's I paid my respects to the woman who hoped that she would never see me again, and the now friendly consultant who was chatting away like an old dear at the market, and made my way down their drive towards my car.

It was Friday afternoon as I came out in the old High Street in Bexhill or Windy Hill as it was known in Saxon times. I chucked my tools in the back of the old banger, threw my work coat over the seat and slammed the large door. I took a deep breath; I was finished for another week.

I looked down to the coast. The sea was shining in the distance like a sheet of grey diamonds under a sapphire blue sky, throwing a trillion scattered shafts of light into the air. A yacht was sailing along, no more than a black curve against the brilliance of the water. The breeze was warm on my face and for a moment, I leant against the side of the car, sunning myself. As I closed my eyes I caught the fresh smell of sea, and in the air I could feel the change of yet another approaching season.

Sweet lord, I thought, over the years I had so many up and downs on this weird and wonderful planet. Man and boy I had survived against all the odds; bent, buckled but still rolling along. As a child most of the nurses at Princess Alice, my local emergency hospital, knew me by my first name. I started early as one of their regulars and when I could cycle I had some bad bicycle accidents (mostly due to living on top of a hill). I progressed to motorcycles and the accidents became more ferocious as I bounced off, up, and over a selection of cars. After moving onto driving cars things became a little safer and so here I was, still wriggling as the world turned. I bet not one of those nurses or doctors would have put money on me reaching adulthood.

I might be one of the last men standing in my trade but besides that nothing much had changed in my long life (which had shot by quicker that two shakes of a lamb's tail). The planet is still fighting itself in countless ways and the papers are still full of the 'next plague' or the 'next killer' that is always out to get us. You know, all the usual bull.

The only thing that I could think about while I was leaning against my car, my faithful friend, was that it had all been worth it. Everything said and done, life with its many pitfalls, was still a glorious ride.

HEARTBEAT

My heart is beating in time with our earth

And my world is turning, always turning,

My life is fleeting, running away from birth,

And my candle is burning, always burning.

AIA

Epilogue

It was late summer 2016. Geese were practicing each morning as autumn rumbled ever closer and soon they would be away to their winter feeding grounds once more. After a long dry summer the trees had decided to shed their leaves early, so they had turned off the sap and sucked up the goodness. The dried up leaves, looking like multi-coloured sweet wrappers, fluttered down onto the roads; a sure sign winter would soon be biting at our heels.

I had been going like the clappers all day and for the last hour I had been working on a beautifully engineered Frister & Rossmann Cub 4, one of the finest Japanese sewing machines from the 1980's. I had done much of my training as a young man on this type of machine; it was my bread and butter. Ben, the chief engineer at Frister's would often give me extra tips on the new models as they came out, and when needed he would use my workshop to dismantle machines. I bent down to pick up the unique offset timing tool, that only fits one shaft, on one machine, but without it you cannot retime the Cub. Imagine a single human hair, one strand, it is about one-thousandth of an inch thick. That is the tolerances sewing machine engineers have to work to and one of the reasons there are so few good ones around, it's just too difficult.

I moved the needle to the top dead centre position then brought the hook round to meet the eye of the needle. Just above the eye is a cut-out called a scarfe, which is almost invisible to the human eye. I flipped down the magnifying lens over my glasses and carefully moved the hook, less than a hairs-breadth, into the scarfe. All this is done by eye and experience. Once sorted I tightened everything up. The hook will silently fly past that tiny cut-out a thousand times a minute and each time it will faultlessly pick up the top thread that has been brought down by the needle. It has to be perfect, there are no near misses in this game. It is 100 percent or the phone is ringing with an irate quilter complaining that her quilt looks more like a cheap import, what with all the missed stitches!

An hour flew by in only moments as my concentration had sucked up the time. A drip of sweat ran down between my shoulder blades as I reached down for my long-handled Singer screwdriver, the first tool for my toolbox given to me by my dad after my training. Back in the day it was over two inches longer but a lifetime of work has worn down the high-carbon vanadium steel and occasionally I carefully regrind the tip and re-magnetise it. In my toolbox is a collection of custom made and precision engineered tools that I have painstakingly built up, Swiss surgical tweezers, Swedish Bacho spanners, German and American hand forged screwdrivers, Sheffield Steel scissors. Many of the tools have been made for me by engineers, long dead now, and some are the latest state-of-the-art electronics for todays computer guided monsters. One toolbox that is priceless to me, and heavy! They say a bad workman blames his tools but it is also true that the best jobs come from the best equipment.

I closed the machine up and re-threaded. I looked at my hands, they were burning red from the blood pumping into every cell after an hour's exercise, lifting, pulling, and twisting the little machine, all to bring her back to life. This was it now, the final test to see if all my work had paid off. I have lived by my word of 'no stitch, no fee' so it was the big test to see if I have earned my pay. Just as I was about to sew, my customer walked in. "Oh you've let your tea get cold, Alex."

"Don't worry, I've been drinking cold tea for years. I quite like it, hot coffee and cold tea." Good name for a book, I thought to myself.

"How is the machine coming along?"

"We're just about to find out." With that I plugged the Frister in, powered her up and ran the first seam along. It was picking up every stitch perfectly but the tension was a little out, puckering the seam. I quickly dropped the bobbin case out, turned the adjusting screw with my thumbnail (that has worn to the perfect shape for the job), popped it back and ran up another seam. It was sweet. I handed the sample to my customer and she smiled. I knew she would be smiling for years when she used the machine, I had done a perfect job - one of the reasons that I don't need to advertise anymore, my happy customers do it for me.

"I'm so glad it was nothing much, Alex." I smile inwardly, knowing that it would be a waste of time to correct her. Mother Nature and Human Nature, both forces that will never change. I had made over 20 different adjustments to get her machine perfect. It's true that sometimes what I do does looks like a magic trick. My hands are flying this way and that while all the time I am engaging the customer in idle banter and then suddenly, POW, the machine is fixed. Forty years of expertise and they think all I did was put a drop of oil on it (which usually has been poured all over it by the helpful husband anyway). "Well, nothing I couldn't handle," I replied to her statement with a broad grin. She paid me and I hit the road.

As I passed Motcombe School, my first school, I noticed there was a new covered bicycle rack but, as most of the kids were too young to ride, it was full of colourful skateboards and scooters with just the odd bicycle, complete with stabilisers. They looked so sweet that I found myself letting out a long "Aaaah." I loved that school and at my next call I was confronted by a seven year old who had an 'in service' day off so was being looked after by granny.

"Alex, may I call you Alex?" She had my full attention now, a bright and bubbly kid with big grey saucepan eyes was looking sternly up at me. She had a guinea pig tucked under each arm and, as I was just about to find out, was on a mission. She didn't wait for me to reply. "Alex, the worst boy in the whole wide world goes to my school and when he found out that I had Ant and Dec, my two guinea pigs here, he told me that in some countries they fry guinea pigs and eat them for breakfast. Well I slapped him and had to take a letter home to mum for my trouble! Mum let me off after I explained what he had said but then I Googled it and found out that in Peru, where I might add, Paddington the Bear comes from, they do eat my babies! No wonder he left. So anyway I have a wonderful plan and that Alex, is where you come in."

By now I was completely mesmerised. "Well, don't keep me in suspense," I said, shaking my hands in excitement. "WHAT'S THE PLAN!"

"I have decided to learn how to sew," she said in a very matter-of-fact voice. "It was me that made Nan phone you to get her machine fixed. Once I can sew I intend to make some superhero capes for Ant and Dec. Then they can fly off to Peru and save all their relatives." She took a deep breath and continued, "Then we can all live here in Eastbourne and we can go down to the beach and play on the sand. How about that?" She finished off with a glorious smile.

"How exciting. I think that's the best idea I've ever heard and I reckon it will work like a dream." I love the way kids see their bright new world with no limits, where everything is possible.

Before long I had the sewing machine humming away and my new protégé had figured out how to sew. She could even use the zig-zag and reverse. I was amazed at how quickly she seemed to pick up all my instructions. I had never taught anyone that young before and I was used to saying everything very slowly and repeating it many times, but that girl was a natural. Each instruction was absorbed and each operation carried out with ease. When I left the house I was topped up with enthusiasm for the sewing. If one little kid was going to save all the guinea pigs in Peru, then the future was bright. My job was done and I was left wondering how she was going to go about training her little pigs! Would she put a big circle around a map of Peru and hold it up to them? I wanted to go back in a few days and see what they looked like in their superhero capes!

Life can be so exciting when you're young and all things are possible. During my 60 years on planet Earth I had discovered so much that I wish they had taught us at school; lessons in life. Wouldn't that be useful? Unfortunately most kids are pushed out of the classroom doors with amazing expectations, often leading disappointingly down just one path; the path of normality. The big problem with life is, it's hard and that can be a big surprise to the kids who suddenly have to stand on their own two feet when they leave home.

Our lives can be both brutal and beautiful at the same time and we have to learn how to handle both as we hurtle through space on this molten blob we call Earth. All life precariously clings to the crust of this world and none of us are properly prepared for our journey. We muddle through the best we can, full of hope and enthusiasm (that sometimes gets a pasting and sometimes a top-up).

As I write, Pope Francis has just made Mother Teresa a saint. Good thing too. I had watched her over the years on her travels around the world and before she shuffled off this mortal coil she had sussed out how to handle problems and find solutions that few of us have ever bettered. She once said something profound that has stayed with me always and I use it as my guide. It is so simple, 'be satisfied with what you have and you will be happier and more fulfilled'. How right she turned out to be, the grass might always be greener on the other side of the fence but it will need twice as much looking after!

Funnily, just as I finished one of my stories, the Sunday Supplement in the Daily Mail had an article by a writer called Chris Baty. He explained how you could write a book in 30 days. I laughed out loud thinking how each of my books takes years to write. Glory Days has taken over four years to put together. Crazy I know but, like a great cake mix, I hope it was worth it in the end.

Well, here we are again. I can't believe I'm coming to the end of another book. It is astonishing really, all these books, and all these tales, but it's been a blast, hasn't it? When I am asked what genre it is I say biographical, again, although most of the tales are not mine. Like Hans Christian Andersen I have just collected them on my travels for everyone else to enjoy. Anyway that about does it, all done and dusted, so now I will leave you my friends and, if I am spared I shall start on my next boundless epic.

I already have some great stories scribbled out while visiting my customers, from Battle of Britain Aces like J. K. Ross D.F.C, who saved us in our darkest hour, to wonderful uplifting tales, but they are all for another day. For now, as the curtains falls once more, I take my bow and wish you a fond farewell.

ALEX ASKAROFF
AN EASTBOURNE LAD BORN AND BRED.

For more information on Alex,
visit www.sewalot.com

TALES FROM THE COAST by Alex Askaroff

Large format paperback 384 pages, illustrated with dozens of pictures
ISBN 978 0-9539410-5-6 **£14.99**

Tales from the Coast continues the series of short true stories in which Alex Askaroff brings both England's history and her people vividly to life. Although they are local stories with Alex's easy writing style and humour they have had world-wide appeal. Alex's American publishers have launched his books in over 40 countries worldwide. and they were some of the first books on digital media like the Apple iPad and Kindle.

Alex Askaroff, a Sussex lad, left a thriving family business in specialty textiles to become a journeyman, travelling our county repairing sewing machines, carrying on a trade that he has known since a child.

This master craftsman has the enthusiasm of a poet and a pure love of story-telling. As Alex brings sewing machines back to life he also picks up local stories, history and gossip. And what stories they are!

The stories in **Tales from the Coast** are as pleasurable as a warm bath after a long hard day. All the stories are inspired by and related by the people who actually lived them. These are real people, no media sensations, just ordinary hard working people who, through their long lives, have had fascinating incidents indelibly burned into their memories.

Tales from the Coast celebrates the spirit of Sussex life, its people, colour and vibrancy. Dorothy tells of her years of hop picking even as the Battle of Britain rages overhead, Sheila tells of her encounter with a jaguar in the jungle far from home, Flo tells of her evacuation as a child and her glorious years on the farm far away from harm.

From the disappearance of Lord Lucan in Uckfield to the Buxted Witch, from William Duke of Normandy to Queen Elizabeth's Eastbourne dressmaker, **Tales from the Coast** is crammed with a fascinating mix of true stories that will have you entranced from start to finish.